Reyita

Reyita

The Life of a Black Cuban Woman in the Twentieth Century

María de los Reyes Castillo Bueno,

as told to her daughter

Daisy Rubiera Castillo

With an introduction by Elizabeth Dore

Translated from the Spanish by Anne McLean

Duke University Press
Durham 2000

© Daisy Rubiera Castillo

First published in North America by Duke University Press,
Box 90660, Durham, NC 27708-0660

Library of Congress Cataloging-in-Publication Data
Castillo Bueno, María de los Reyes, 1902–1997
[Reyita, sencillamente. English]
Reyita : the life of a Black Cuban woman in the twentieth century
p. cm.
ISBN 0-8223-2579-9 (cloth: alk.paper) – ISBN 0-8223-2593-4 (paper: alk.paper)
1. Reyes Castillo Bueno, María de los, 1902–1997. 2. Blacks–Cuba–Biography
3. Cuba–Race relations. 4. Cuba–History–1895- I. Rubiera Castillo, Daisy.
II. Title.
F1789.N3 R89 2000
972.9106'092–dc21
[B] 99-087007

and in the UK by the Latin American Bureau,
1 Amwell Street, London ECIR IUL

Published in Spanish in 1996 by Prolibros
Palacio del Segundo Cabo
O'Relly no 4, esquina a Tacón
La Habana, Cuba
and the World Data Research Center
Calle E No. 158 4to Pios, Esquina a 9na
Plaza de la Revolucíon
La Habana, Cuba

Translator: Anne McLean

Contents

Introduction

Afro-Cuban history from below

It is commonly said that people make history, but not under conditions of their own choosing; they make history under conditions they inherit from the past.[1] *Reyita* is the story of a woman who did *not* make history because of the conditions she inherited from the past. *Reyita* is about the life of an ordinary black woman who witnessed the brutal suppression of Afro-Cuban politics in the early 20th century. The massacre of black political leaders and of thousands of ordinary blacks in 1912, and its violent aftermath, terrified the entire Afro-Cuban population into submission. Never again did Afro-Cubans organize to fight for racial equality and justice.

Reyita tells a story that has never been told in public before. She recounts growing up poor, black and female in Oriente Province. Her account is very personal; it is also very political in the sense that her personal life was conditioned by the politics of the era in which she lived. But without knowledge of Afro-Cuban history we fail to make sense of the politics, or mostly the anti-politics, of Reyita's life and times.

Reyita's life, as she describes it, falls into three periods that coincide with watersheds in Afro-Cuban history. Reyita begins her testimony by describing how her ancestors and later she herself participated in Afro-Cuban struggles for freedom and equality. The years between 1868 and 1921 were times of widespread Afro-Cuban political action for social change. First, slaves and free blacks in massive numbers voluntarily joined the struggle for Cuban independence from Spain, in large part to end slavery. Then, following abolition in 1886, and the end of Spanish colonialism in 1898, Afro-Cubans mobilized again to struggle for equality in the new Republic.[2] Reyita tells of this period largely through the experiences of her grandmother and mother who participated in the anti-colonial struggles as noncombatants. Reyita's description of this era, especially of Cuba's independence wars and their aftermath, is not the one routinely offered. Whereas Cuban historians present the wars as a male experience, and one that generated black pride among its Afro-Cuban protagonists, Reyita's account focuses on the female experience of war, which was far from glorious.

Reyita vividly recalls the next defining moment in Afro-Cuban history: the 1912 massacre of the Independent Colored Party (the Partido Independiente de Color, or PIC). The creation of the PIC in 1908 followed a decade of black political exclusion. Blacks felt betrayed after independence because they had played a leading role in the anti-colonial struggle but were denied the rewards of citizenship whites enjoyed. Increasingly frustrated by the failure to achieve social and political equality with whites, Afro-Cubans formed autonomous organizations to redress racial injustice. The PIC, one of the first black parties in the hemisphere, focused on racial equality and working class demands.[3]

The PIC rejected the prevailing ideology that Cuba was a racial democracy. The white Cuban elite and some black leaders held that Cuban society was characterized by racial equality. They maintained that in the absence of legal segregation, through hard work and clean-living, deserving blacks could achieve equality with whites. If blacks did not progress socially and economically, it was not the result of discrimination and racism: it was their own fault. From this point of view, the fact that the upper classes were exclusively white and the lower classes largely black had nothing to do with social policy and racist ideology. Instead, it was evidence that whites were naturally superior and blacks naturally inferior. A less racist rendering of the myth of racial democracy legitimated the idea that blacks suffered from cultural, educational and economic deprivation, and needed to be uplifted *before* they could participate as full citizens in the political life of the country.[4]

The PIC rejected these views of Cuban society. Their leaders proclaimed that it was white racism and whites' monopoly on political and economic power, not black inferiority, that prevented blacks from gaining 'their rightful share' of power, wealth and jobs.[5] The demands of the PIC included full political equality for Afro-Cuban men and their proportional representation in public sector jobs. This platform had widespread appeal among blacks, and the Party quickly established a nationwide organization and mass membership.

The Party's success brought forth a violent reaction from the state. The Party was outlawed in 1910, and the government launched a campaign branding the Party as a black racist conspiracy against whites. In 1912 leaders of the PIC organized an armed protest calling for legalization of the Party. In retaliation, the Cuban Army massacred the leaders and thousands of followers of the PIC, bringing an end to Afro-Cubans' challenge to white rule. The slaughter of 1912 signalled 'the end of black Cuban radicalism'.[6]

For its part, along with repressing black movements, the Cuban state actively pursued a policy that sought to 'improve' the island's so-called racial stock through whitening. The government subsidized the immigration of whites, particularly Spaniards, in order to reduce the proportion of blacks in the population and to increase the possibility of 'whitening' by way of mixed-race marriages.

Reyita witnessed the birth and violent demise of the PIC. As a child she lived in La Maya, where the Party had a large following among peasants and workers. Reyita's aunt was

3

President of the Party's Committee of Ladies, and Reyita remembered the comings and goings of the Party's leaders, as well as the violence of the massacre.[7] Here too, Reyita's telling of events gives us a view of female experience that has been hidden from history. Whereas historical sources provide few clues about women's participation in the PIC, it is interesting to note that in Reyita's household her aunt, not her uncle, was the Party militant.

Reyita participated in one of the last Afro-Cuban collective efforts for what could be called loosely 'black liberation'. After the 1912 massacre, when many Afro-Cubans abandoned hope of living with dignity in Cuba, Reyita and others in Oriente joined Marcus Garvey's back-to-Africa movement, the Universal Negro Improvement Association.[8] In 1921 the Cuban state stepped in again and crushed the movement. This marked the end of Reyita's participation in organized race politics.

With their possibilities for collective action blocked, Afro-Cubans developed alternative goals and strategies. Many Afro-Cuban men joined trade unions and political parties, particularly the Cuban Communist Party. A few middle-class Afro-Cuban women participated in the suffragette movement. Being a poor black woman, these avenues of political action were for the most part closed to Reyita. Like other women of her class and colour, Reyita devoted herself mostly to community forms of self-help and mutual assistance that Aline Helg describes as 'constituting a kind of alternative way of life.'[9] In addition, Reyita dedicated herself to upward mobility.

Reyita's life, as she recounts it, from the 1920s until the triumph of the revolution in 1959, was a never-ending struggle to earn enough money to 'make something' of her children. The struggle for family advancement is the centerpiece of her story. Reyita was driven to improve herself and her children, as measured by a society from which, as a poor, black woman, she was largely excluded. To realize her ambitions, Reyita 'married white' to lighten the skin colour of her offspring. She dedicated herself relentlessly to street vending and to other shoestring ventures, and to installment-buying of things she could barely afford. She was submissive to a white husband she disdained, even though he thwarted her ambition and that of their children at every turn because he was racist – or so she suspected. She indebted herself up to the eyeballs to buy things – like a living room suite – that she enjoyed showing off. These aspirations created almost unbearable tensions in her life.

Reyita's life shows the multiple contradictions of living in a society with a myth of racial democracy, and on top of that a society where Afro-Cubans had learned painful lessons about what was politically possible and impossible. Although Reyita was denigrated by her own mother on account of her colour, Reyita herself subscribed to aspects of the ideology of white superiority/black inferiority; she strove to improve the race – at least her family – through whitening. Furthermore, she put into practice the official ideology that Afro-Cubans could get ahead through hard work. And she was so successful in her upward mobility that her story might seem to confirm what she otherwise explicitly rejected: the myth of racial democracy. On the other hand, Reyita displayed great pride in her African heritage. Her quasi-political action took the form of practicing African religions that were reconstructed in Cuba.

With movements for racial justice hounded out of the political sphere, Afro-Cuban race politics went underground. It flourished in popular religious practices, such as *santería*. As Helg argues, *santería* constituted 'a strand of "politics" that can only be understood as such in the context of Afro-Cuban history'.[10] In the 1920s whites demonized *brujos* (male *santería* priests). Because the state jailed alleged *brujos*, Afro-Cuban religious practices came to be associated in people's consciousness with racial militancy. Consequently, in the absence of formal race politics, *santería* constituted a politics of the oppressed. Understanding *santería* in this light, it becomes clear that Reyita challenged the values of white Cuban society by practicing Afro-Cuban religions. Her spiritualism and healing contributed to preserving African pride, and was a form of engagement in race politics. Moreover, as most *brujos* were male, Reyita's religious practices may have gone some way towards challenging the gender order within the Afro-Cuban community.

The different aspects of Reyita's life might be construed as inconsistent. The fact that seemingly incompatible ideas and behaviours, for instance marrying white and practicing *santería*, sat side-by-side in her life, demonstrate that in their struggle to live with dignity Afro-Cubans adopted an assortment of strategies.

The revolution of 1959 unleashed sweeping changes in Cuba. To create the conditions for socialism, the government dismantled the capitalist state and economy, and drastically reduced class differences. Keeping in mind that a large part of Reyita's life was dedicated to upward mobility, it is a testament to the popular support the revolutionary forces enjoyed, especially among Afro-Cubans, that two of her sons joined Fidel's 26th of July Movement. Reyita speaks proudly of this episode in her family history, and with pride tempered by grief about one son's death, a victim of counter-revolutionary sabotage. Other than these memories, Reyita says surprisingly little about how the revolution changed her life. Reyita lived through one of the decisive events of the 20th century and yet she has almost nothing to say about her life during the revolution.

Reyita speaks about racism in the revolution, albeit very briefly. 'These days you don't have to worry about the colour of your skin,' sits uneasily alongside, 'I know of quite a few people who still have serious racial problems...', which she follows up with some telling examples. Her contradictory statements reflect contradictions of the revolution. Racism in

Cuba declined precipitously after 1959.[11] The revolutionary government proclaimed that racism was a product of capitalism and U.S. imperialism, and that socialism would solve the problem of racism. With this analysis, the revolutionary government downplayed the question of race, and actively discouraged Afro-Cubans from thinking about themselves as in any way different from white Cubans. Lack of official attention to racism may be part of the reason why Cuba has failed to end racial discrimination.

Race

So far I have used the words race, white, black and Afro-Cuban unproblematically. But they are very problematic terms. Therefore, I turn to a discussion of how we might usefully think about race, particularly to shed light on Reyita's life and times.

Race is not a category grounded in our genes; nevertheless, race is very important as an ideology of human difference.[12] People include or exclude others based on their perception of physical difference. Therefore, because people behave *as if* races exist, race does exist, but as a *social* category rooted in supposed natural differences, not as a biological category rooted in verifiable genetic differences.[13]

Race and racism as we know them in modern Latin America, the Caribbean and North America are largely the product of European conquest and colonization. Europeans differentiated themselves from the peoples they conquered and enslaved on the basis of observable shared physical attributes, which they called race. Peter Wade calls shared traits – skin colour, hair type, and facial features – physical 'cues'. These particular physical cues became racial signifiers of superiority and inferiority and played their part in a historical process of political domination. Furthermore, colonization served to legitimate the idea that

7

social and cultural differences among groups are caused by natural physical differences. However, in our effort to lay bare the ideological roots of race and racism, there may be a danger in going too far towards jettisoning physicality. The point is that how we interpret certain physical traits is a product of history and of social conditioning.

In the case of people of African descent living outside Africa, race is an idea forged in the history of slavery, but not limited to that history. As George Reid Andrews argues in the case of Brazil, race and racism are continually recreated in the context of changing social conditions.[14] This partly explains why 'black' identity is different across the Americas. In the United States, historically a 'black' identity was assigned to any person with traceable African ancestry, what was sometimes called 'the one drop of black blood rule'. As a consequence, the U.S. has a largely binary black-white colour code. However, in many countries of Latin America there is a continuum of black racial categories that originally purported to describe varying mixtures of black and white ancestry, and that came to be associated with shades of skin tone. As a consequence of different colour codes, a person considered mulatto (mixed race) or white in Cuba, might be 'black' in the U.S.[15] The important point here is that the meanings of black and white are not fixed; they vary according to the social context.

It would be an exaggeration to say that understanding race helps us 'to make sense of' racism in Reyita's life and times, for the simple reason that frequently it is impossible 'to make sense of' – to logically explain – racism. Racism by its very nature frequently defies logic. Nevertheless, it might be fair to say that understanding what race is goes some way to sensitizing us to racism in Reyita's changing world.

Reyita describes a tripartite colour code that characterized Oriente when she was coming of age. For instance, separate social and political organizations existed for black, brown (mulatto), and white Cubans. It is apparent that the racial order she describes was considerably different from the more binary divide between black and white that existed then – and now – in the United States. The differences in race politics between the U.S. and Cuba in the early 20th century were products, among other things, of black Cubans' massive participation in their anti-colonial struggle, and an interaction between race and class in Cuba that allowed some Afro-Cubans a certain level of social mobility.

Reyita's story tells us more about how racism infected everyday life than we can learn from other historical accounts. Historians have often characterized the first decade of the 20th century as a period when Afro-Cubans manifested pride in their 'blackness', largely because of their heroic contributions to the Cuban Wars of Independence. But this is not the world Reyita knew. Reyita describes how her mulatta mother and sisters abused her because her skin colour was darker than theirs. In these memories, as in others throughout her testimony, *Reyita* provides a rich vein of information about the varied and contradictory nature of Afro-Cuban identities. Reyita's narrative is replete with the ambiguities of race in everyday life. Because the paradoxes of Reyita's experiences of race are not excised from her narrative, she helps us dispose of overly simple understandings of Afro-Cuban identity, or what has come to be called *Afro-Cubanidad.*

'Waking up'

Reyita's story highlights how race, class and gender were inextricably woven into the fabric of her life. One aspect of the testimonial genre in general, and of her story in particular, is that through the narration of experiences we, the reader, can appreciate the subtle and not-so-subtle interconnectedness of race, class and gender that historians often find hard to decipher as well as to explain.

Reyita's life from the time of her marriage until sometime in the 1940s conformed closely to a stereotype of Afro-Caribbean womanhood. Reyita was submissive to her husband, to the point of putting on his socks while he was lying in bed in the mornings: 'He didn't demand it of me, I did it willingly and for a long time.' She had about a dozen children and dedicated her life to hard work in order to make something of them. Reyita was the problem solver in the household; when extra money was needed she figured out a way to earn it.

Then, when she joined the Popular Socialist Party in the 1940s, her ideas began to change. She joined the Party because it fought for equality between blacks and whites and between men and women. In the Party, Reyita mostly did 'women's work'. She organized *fiestas*, held bake sales, and helped out in the Party's dressmaking academy. Reyita sees this as a period of awakening. 'I led a very active life within the Party. Rubiera [her husband] didn't like it at all, but I paid no attention to him...I was waking up, you know. Waking up from the blindness caused by my naiveté'. Although Reyita never uses the word feminist, she is describing a feminist awakening. However, the family moved away and Reyita lost her political connections.

Another turning point in Reyita's awakening was of a very different order. She made up her mind to work hard and save money in order to have electricity installed in the house so that she could buy a radio. As she says, '[that] episode caused an important transformation in me, a big change occurred in my life: my independence! After that, I could do things without telling the old man [Rubiera], I'd broken the tradition of submission to the man of the house.' The stark difference in these two defining moments in Reyita's feminist awakening should alert us to the fallacy of trying to explain the rise of gender consciousness in clear-cut ways.

'I sacrificed everything. I sacrificed myself as a woman to be just a mother...' In these few words Reyita communicates the plight of poor black women in Oriente in the pre-revolutionary period. What Reyita does not say here, but which she implies, is that she wanted to be much more than just a mother. Reyita wanted to be many things; she wanted to fulfil her ambitions and dreams as a person. But in the context of poverty, racism and sexism she had to sacrifice herself 'to be *just* a mother'. Her next sentence lays bare more of the contradictions of her life. She tells her daughter, 'I started to build a life independent of your dad in order to be able, with my own efforts, to give all of you what I yearned for: an education, personal development, minding the environment...' Frankly that last – the environment – strikes a distinctly odd chord. But the important point here is that Reyita did not build an independent life for herself to realize her dreams of becoming a poet or an activist. She did it to give her children what she yearned for for them. Even in her independence Reyita could not get away from being 'just a mother.'

Reflecting on the gains of the Cuban revolution, such as universal education and employment, and the virtual elimination of poverty, at this point in her narrative one cannot help but think that the next generation of Afro-Cuban women probably did not suffer in ways Reyita did. The revolution subordinated the demands of women, particularly feminist demands, on a range of issues including machismo and men's reluctance to share housework;[16] nevertheless, socialism in Cuba was associated with sweeping improvements in most women's lives. If Reyita's children had been provided for in the ways children were in the revolution, with high quality education, health care, housing and food, possibly Reyita could have been more than 'just a mother.' But Reyita says little about her life and the lives of her children after the revolution. Even though the revolution is conspicuous by its absence from the testimony, speaking as a woman after more than three decades of socialist transformation, Reyita's ideas about sexism and racism reflect the values of revolutionary society.

Testimonies

The testimonial genre has been the subject of a debate over issues of authenticity, truth-telling and who is representing whom and for what purposes. The controversy surrounding the testimonial form began with the publication in Cuba in 1966 of Esteban Montejo's *The Autobiography of a Runaway Slave*, as told to Miguel Barnet.[17] *Reyita* has been called its sequel. The testimonial debate gathered steam over the next twenty years,[18] and culminated in 1999 with the uproar over what was true and what was not in *I, Rigoberta Menchú: An Indian Woman in Guatemala*.[19] The accusation that Rigoberta Menchú's testimony contained half-truths and lies, included in the text for political purposes, transformed a scholarly debate about the nature of the testimonial genre into a political debate about the politics of the Left. In light of this furore, it would be unwise to read testimonials unproblematically, as true life stories.

The 1980s was the boom for Latin American testimonial literature. In the context of Central America's revolutionary upheavals, activists, most notably Rigoberta Menchú, recounted their experiences for a political purpose: to raise awareness of and build support for their struggles. At that time most academic writers argued that testimonials were 'real'. They maintained that testimonial writings made the invisible visible, and gave voice to those who previously had been silenced. Academics read testimonials as quasi-historical sources that presented the authentic voices of oppressed people who were protagonists in or witnesses to the events they narrated.[20]

After postmodernism took hold in the academy a number of scholars changed their minds about testimonials. They decided that it was naive to think that testimonials empowered the narrator to speak directly to a world from which they had been excluded. The new orthodoxy viewed the author/editor of the testimony as a powerful intermediary between marginalized storyteller and elite reader, and consequently as the person who controlled the text. Issues such as the ambiguity of texts, the shifting nature of truth, the problems of representation and the position of the narrative voice dominated the discussion about testimonials in the second phase.[21] At risk of over-simplifying the debate, one could say that in the first phase scholars read testimonials as authentic histories of the oppressed, and in the second phase more as fictionalized accounts of the downtrodden.[22]

In my view, the testimony can be best understood neither as history nor as fiction, but as an extension of the oral tradition of storytelling.[23] The storyteller in pre-literate societies preserved and transmitted collective memories; the testimonial narrator aims to do the same, often with the express purpose of raising consciousness so readers will become active in movements for progressive social change. However, there are major differences between the storytelling and the testimonial traditions. In particular, in the oral tradition neither storyteller nor listener pretended that the story represented verifiable evidence; in the testimonial tradition there was an assumption on both sides that it did.

The major conclusion I draw from the controversy over testimonial writing is that readers would do well to reflect on how testimonies are produced. If, as readers, we analyze the process of production, we might come to a better understanding of who is saying what to whom and for what purposes. Analysis of the production process draws attention to a number of issues including: Why is the storyteller telling her/his story? Does the testimony transmit memories of a collective or of an individual nature? Is the voice mostly that of the story-teller,

13

or that of the author/interviewer, often referred to as the interlocutor? For whom is the testimony intended? Why, how and by whom was the testimony published? In the case of *I, Rigoberta Menchú*, as a consequence of the controversy over truthfulness, there is a large literature that readers can draw on to answer these questions.[24]

In the case of *Reyita* we have little to go on. *Reyita* was published in Havana in 1997, during what in Cuba was called 'the Special Period'. Special, because Cuba had been the beneficiary – and the victim – of considerable Soviet economic assistance from 1961 to 1989. Then, following the collapse of the Soviet bloc, Cuba lost its traditional trading partners, export markets and foreign assistance. Consequently, the Cuban economy contracted sharply until 1994. In the second half of the 1990s, although the economy slowly began to recover, the economic situation remained very difficult. In the Special Period, not only did the Cuban state exercise monopoly control over the publication of books and newspapers, as it had since the early 1960s, but few books of any kind were published because of shortages of paper. *Reyita* was one of the very few to see the light. That *Reyita* was a finalist for the Casa de las Américas prize, Cuba's highest cultural award, tells us something, but far from enough, about how public culture was constituted in Cuba, and whose voice counted.

One might logically have expected that the natural audience for this unique testimony of an Afro-Cuban woman would be Cubans, particularly Afro-Cubans, living in Cuba. But that was not to be, at least not up until the time I wrote this introduction in July 2000. *Reyita* did not circulate widely in Cuba, and was available only at 'dollar shops'– stores where merchandise was sold in U.S. dollars, not Cuban pesos. This, combined with the paper shortage, undoubtedly go some way towards explaining the book's small circulation in Cuba. In addition, and here I return to where I began, because of conditions inherited from the past, Afro-Cubans might have had even less access to *Reyita* than white Cubans. Most people who left Cuba, at least until the 1980s, were upper- and middle-class white Cubans fleeing the egalitarian and redistributive policies of a socialist state, among other things. Afro-Cubans, as a whole, remained on the island to build a socialist society and to enjoy its fruits. In one of the ironies of history, during the Special Period white Cuban émigrés, Miami-Cubans, sent remittances to relatives in Cuba, subsidizing their standard of living; so white Cubans, more than Afro-Cubans, had money to spend at the dollar shops. More importantly, although the majority of Cubans are black, Afro-Cubans remained under-represented in the upper echelons of power and over-represented in the lower echelons of society.

During the revolution Afro-Cubans came a long way, but, as Reyita says, 'there's still a long way to go.'

Elizabeth Dore
July 2000

Elizabeth Dore is Reader in Latin American History at the University of Portsmouth (UK). She has written extensively in the fields of modern Latin American history, gender studies and social theory. She is the author of *The Peruvian Mining Industry: Growth, Stagnation and Crisis* (1988), editor of *Gender Politics in Latin America: Debates in Theory and Practice* (1997) and co-editor of *Hidden Histories of Gender and the State in Latin America* (2000). She is completing a book on patriarchy and peonage in rural Nicaraguan history.

[1] In *The Eighteenth Brumaire of Louis Bonaparte*, Marx wrote 'Men make their own history, but they do not make it just as they please; they do not make it under circumstances chosen by themselves, but under circumstances directly encountered, given and transmitted from the past.' Karl Marx/Frederick Engels, *Collected Works*, Vol. 11 (New York: International Publishers, 1979), 103. For a discussion about how and when people make history see Deborah Levenson-Estrada, *Trade Unionists Against Terror: Guatemala City, 1954-1985* (Chapel Hill: University of North Carolina Press, 1994) 5-7.

[2] From the defeat of Spain in 1898 to the revolution of 1959 Cuba was a neo-colony of the United States. In 1898 Washington established a protectorate over Cuba and the island was ruled for four years by U.S. military governors. In 1902 the U.S. granted independence to Cuba, with the proviso that Washington could intervene in the country's domestic and foreign affairs. This 'right' of intervention was formalized in the Platt Amendment. In 1933 the Cuban government declared the Platt Amendment null and void.

[3] My discussion of this period and of the Partido Independiente de Color is drawn primarily from Aline Helg, *Our Rightful Share: The Afro-Cuban Struggle for Equality, 1886-1912* (Chapel Hill: University of North Carolina Press, 1994).

[4] Helg, 4.

[5] Helg, 10.

[6] Helg, 21.

[7] For another account of the massacre see Helg, 210-211.

[8] Further research on Garveyism in Cuba is needed, as historians argue that Garveyism had little support. See Bernardo García Domínguez, 'Garvey and Cuba,' in Rupert Lewis and Patrick Bryan, eds., *Garvey: His Work and Impact* (Trenton, NJ: Africa World Press, 1988), 299-305; and Judith Stein, *The World of Marcus Garvey: Race and Class in Modern Society* (Baton Rouge: Louisiana State University Press, 1986).

[9] Helg, 15.

[10] Helg, 238- 48.

[11] Mirta Ojito, 'Best of Friends, Worlds Apart,' *The New York Times on the Web*, 5 June 2000.

[12] At the end of the 20th century, with scientific breakthroughs in genetics, most geneticists reached the conclusion that races do not exist. This means that, in the words of Peter Wade, 'the idea of race is just that – an idea.' Peter Wade, *Race and Ethnicity in Latin America* (London and Chicago: Pluto Press, 1997), 13.

[13] Wade,14.

[14] George Reid Andrews, *Blacks and Whites in São Paulo, Brazil, 1888-1988* (Madison, WI: University of Wisconsin Press, 1991), 3-22.

[15] Ojito, 'Best of Friends, Worlds Apart;' and, Esmeralda Santiago, *When I was Puerto Rican* (New York: Vintage Books, 1993).

[16] Maxine Molyneux, 'State, Gender and Institutional Change: The Federación de Mujeres Cubanas,' in Elizabeth Dore and Maxine Molyneux, eds., *Hidden Histories of Gender and the State in Latin America* (Durham & London: Duke University Press, 2000), 291-321.

[17] Esteban Montejo, *The Autobiography of a Runaway Slave* (Basingstoke: Macmillan, 1993). For analysis of the ambiguities of the author-narrator relation in the Barnet/Montejo collaboration see, Elzbieta Sklodowska, 'Spanish American Testimonial Novel: Some Afterthoughts', in *The Real Thing: Testimonial Discourse and Latin America*, Georg M. Gugelberger, ed., (Durham & London: Duke University Press, 1996), 84-100.

[18] See, Georg M. Gugelberger, ed., *The Real Thing*.

[19] Elizabeth Burgos-Debray, *I, Rigoberta Menchú: An Indian Woman in Guatemala* (London and New York: Verso, 1984), translated by Ann Wright. For David Stoll's critical reassessment of Rigoberta Menchú's testimony, see *Rigoberta Menchú and the Story of All Poor Guatemalans* (Boulder: Westview Press, 1998). For contributions to the debate see, 'If Truth Be Told: A Forum on Stoll and Menchú', *Latin American Perspectives*, 26:6 (November 1999).

[20] John Beverly, 'The Margin at the Center: On Testimonio (Testimonial Narrative)' in *The Real Thing*, Gugelberger, ed., 23-41, article first published in 1989; and George Yúdice, 'Testimonio and Postmodernism,' *Latin American Perspectives*, 18: 3 (Summer 1991): 15-31.

[21] Georg M. Gugelberger, 'Introduction,' in *The Real Thing*, Gugelberger, ed., 1-19. Gugelberger argues there was a third phase in the debate that represented a kind of synthesis of the two earlier viewpoints. See chapters by Alberto Morairas, Gareth Williams and Jorge Sanjines in *The Real Thing*.

[22] The two chapters by John Beverly, 'The Margin at the Center' and 'The Real Thing,' exemplify the shift. In *The Real Thing*, Gugelberger, ed., 1-19; 266-286.

[23] Jan Rus, 'Introduction,' 'If Truth Be Told', 8-9.

[24] 'If Truth Be Told'.

*Only when one has inspiration, warmth, a friendly
outstretched hand and a sympathetic intellect
to turn to, is it possible to overcome obstacles and express
emotions.
For me, inspiration, warmth, hand and intellect have
many names. Some are: Roberto Fernández
Retamar, Aníbal Argüelles, Alberto Pedro,
Georgina Herrera, Sonnia Moro.
To these, and to those unnamed,
thank you.*

To Reyita,
whose mere presence unites,
I cede the floor

Chapter I

Rocking in the wicker chair,
a tumult of memories come:
long dead sorrows,
joys, ideas;
the present fades,
and the ocean grows,
when the suns and moons of memory
flash on your inward eye[1]

White hair, black skin. Who am I?

I am Reyita, a regular, ordinary person. A natural person, respectful, helpful, decent, affectionate and very independent. For my mother, it was an embarrassment, that I – of her four daughters – was the only black one. I always felt the difference between us, because she didn't have as much affection for me as she did for my sisters. She rebuked me in hurtful ways and was always saying: 'that black one, that *jocicúa.'[2]* I always felt she rejected me.

I was the victim of terrible discrimination on my mother's part. And if you add what was then the case in Cuba, you can understand why I never wanted a black husband. I had good reason, you know. I didn't want to have children as black as me, so that no one would look down on them, no one would harass and humiliate them. Oh, God only knows...! I didn't want my children to suffer what I'd had to suffer. That's why I wanted to *'adelantar la raza'*,[3] that's why I married a white man.

There was a time when I suffered enormously on *Día de los Reyes*.[4] It was so sad for the poor to make their children believe in the Three Wise Men, and not to be able – even though they'd been good and well-behaved – to indulge them with what they'd asked for in their little letters. And it was heartbreaking to have to dash their hopes. How lovingly they'd put the herbs, water and candies beside their tiny shoes with their letters inside! I couldn't help crying when I saw their sad faces, disappointed because what they found in no way resembled what they'd asked for.

Día de los Reyes was really hard for me, even more so because it's my birthday: I was born one 6th of January, in 1902, that's why they called me María de los Reyes, Reyita for short. That was at 'El Desengaño', a farm on the outskirts of La Maya, a village in Oriente province, in eastern Cuba. My surnames should be Castillo Hechavarría,[5] because my mother had the last name of my grandma's owner who was also her father. But all us children felt such hatred towards that family – who we didn't even know – that my brother Pepe decided we'd change it to Bueno. It wasn't difficult: none of us were officially registered.

But for a long time now *Día de los Reyes* has been full of happiness for me. My house seems tiny when it's so full of family, who come to bring me cheer and encourage me when I say I want to live till the 6th of January 2002. And also, how about the neighbours who, every year at midnight on the 5th of January, serenade me and bring a cake and we all eat it. Yes, at midnight! And it's never done me any harm, we dance and sing for a while. Now I feel myself to be a happy woman on my birthday. That's why I've sworn to die on this very day, when I turn 100.

Happiness was more fleeting during the first fifty or sixty years of my life. Let me see, how to stitch together my ideas to tell you about all that. It's like living it all over again, reopening wounds I've wanted to keep closed, even though on some sleepless nights it all runs through my mind like a movie.

My Grandma flew away

From my earliest years there are some things I haven't forgotten, subjects of conversation among the grown-ups I overheard – at four or five years of age – from the yard or the kitchen, because in my day kids weren't allowed to sit with the grown-ups while they chatted. I remember those things clearly, because they were so sad and painful.

My grandmother's name was Antonina, although everyone called her Tatica; she died in 1917. She had beautiful skin, not black-black but a very deep dark shade. She was plump, of medium height; she had lovely hair and wore it in an attractive style: she parted it in the middle and made two braids at the front and two at the back, then she'd pin them up behind her ears; she had a beautiful smile. She loved headscarves but she only wore them for going out. If only you could have seen how pretty she looked in her long, full skirts with flowers, polka-dots or stripes. She wore short blouses called *chambras* and boots that buttoned up on one side. Tatica was very funny, she always had some joke to tell. She didn't like them hitting me so she was forever covering up for the naughty things I did. All in all, she was a grandmother who was crazy about her grandchildren and went out of her way for them. She was wonderful, my grandma!

Tatica told us her family came from a little village in a place called Cabinda,[6] they were Quicongos[7] and they grew manioc and coffee and also wove with raffia. The men of the village made canoes, drums and various wooden utensils. My great-

23

grandmother on my mother's side was called Sabina and she had seven children: six girls and a boy.

One evening, when the family was at home, having finished working in the fields, and the children were playing, they suddenly heard explosions and shouting. It was a group of white men with guns who were attacking the village, burning the houses and capturing women and men, killing children and old people. It was a terrible massacre. My great-grandmother saw her husband and son vanish; she tried as hard as she could to defend the girls but they beat her and took the three oldest – Tatica, Casilda and Nestora. My grandmother never forgot her mother's screams, never understood why they didn't take her too, because she wasn't that old. Tatica never even knew if she'd survived.

After such horror came the long march to the steamer – as she used to say – she never managed to figure out how long it lasted. They tied them to each other so they couldn't escape. She was tied up with Casilda, Nestora was a little bit behind. On the way they'd be beaten if they fell down from exhaustion or thirst.

The ship that took them from Africa was crammed with men, women and even children, though not many... She said they were the ones the whites couldn't wrench out of their mothers' arms. Since it was so full, there was some problem, and although Tatica didn't know precisely what was wrong, they started throwing men overboard – the oldest, the most frail. What an outrage! Just hearing about it made you want to cry, and even now my eyes well up with tears and you feel tremendously indignant because they threw them overboard alive, with no compassion whatsoever.

When they reached land, Tatica and my aunts didn't know where they were, it was much later that they found out this was Cuba. They took them to a big hut where they were fed and had water thrown over them. Of course, they couldn't understand anything the whites said, only later they realized the water was to clean them up a little; not out of goodness, of course, but rather so they'd look better when they were put up for sale.

I never understood exactly how the three of them managed to stay together; when she talked about it she'd give thanks to someone I didn't know – and who I later understood was their God – that a person from the Hechavarría family bought all three of them. It was a wretched sight – my grandmother told me – when they sold members of a family separately: the mothers and children would be screaming and screaming and all they could understand was they had to be quiet if they didn't want to receive more blows.

They were made to work very hard at the estate where they were taken. Cutting and gathering sugar cane, weeding. They also had to press the cane in machines called *cunyayas* to extract the juice, for the masters to drink or to make into sugar candy. The Hechavarrías also bought other Africans, there were about fifteen or twenty altogether on the plantation. One of them was young and strong and not from my grandmother's village. His name was Basilio and he and Tatica fell in love.

They lived together secretly so the masters wouldn't find out. Although my grandmother didn't want to have children – and she took preventative infusions of herbs and roots – she got pregnant and had a daughter they named Socorro, who had to work very hard from a very young age. Later my mother was born, she had to work as a slave doing housework for the masters, even though this was after the *law of free wombs*.[8]

My mother wasn't Basilio's daughter, but one of my grandmother's masters was her father. The slaves couldn't resist when the masters wanted to take advantage of them. It would have cost them a whipping and the stocks. There was an immoral hypocrisy in those men: on the one hand they looked down on them, but when it came to rape they didn't care what colour their skin was.

After the abolition of slavery in 1886, Tatica went to live in a little hut which Basilio built on a tiny piece of land he was given. And there, while undergoing terrible hardships, wresting from the earth what they needed to live, her third daughter Nestora was born. They worked very hard. When Basilio joined up with the independence forces in the war of 1895,[9] Tatica took to the hills with him.

I used to look enviously at her gold chain, though she also wore coloured necklaces, which I later knew to be from her religion. Tatica didn't like Catholicism, she was very superstitious and believed in life after death. I remember what my grandmother used to say about Africans who lived far away from their countries. She said their spirits returned to their lands when they died. I couldn't go to her funeral because I didn't live in La Maya anymore, but I remember when the news got to Banes. I cried so much! But when I calmed down and closed my eyes I seemed to see her rise up to the sky and fly through the clouds, on the way back to her native land, towards her beloved, never forgotten Africa, which I learned to love too from all the stories she told us.

Blacks with blacks

This love for her homeland that my grandma instilled in me had a big influence on my decision to join Marcus Garvey's[10] movement – to go to Africa – tired of being discriminated against for being black. In Cueto, I'd sneak into the house of Molvaina Grand, Miss Molly, for the meetings she held on Sundays with her husband, Charles Clark. They ran the organization and I loved talking with them. I was very restless – an adolescent, after all – and I always liked to be involved in something. The Jamaicans were all fired up about going to

Africa. After a few meetings, I had at least as much enthusiasm as them and I got fully involved in the movement. We were sure things would be different over there: blacks with blacks, they had to be different! We were going to be one big family and, most importantly, without racial discrimination.

Miss Molly took in washing and ironing, but only stiff collared white shirts; she also made delicious candies to sell: *yemitas de coco* and others called *cocoanut*. The *yemitas de coco* were easy to make with grated coconut and sugar. You grated the coconut and drained off the milk, which you put to boil with sugar, cinnamon sticks, anise, vanilla and then a pinch of salt; you let it thicken till it was like cane-syrup; let it cool and then you'd beat it with a wooden spatula in the same pot. When it started to harden, you emptied it out onto a board and kneaded it, then shaped the *yemitas* and arranged them on another board to finish drying. The *cocoanut* was harder: it was made with grated coconut, sugar, cinnamon, anise and vanilla, something like a *cocá*,[11] and when it was thick you beat it with a wooden spatula, then you'd scoop them out with a little wooden mould and set them out on a board to dry. These I could never get right, I never knew exactly when to start beating it: they always went sugary on me.

At those Sunday meetings Mr.. Clark presented information about Africa, African life, and about the amount of land we'd have available when we got there. When I listened to him I'd remember all my grandmother's stories.

I was very active, they gave me the job of visiting other black people to invite them to join; I got a lot of my friends and a few of my black relatives enthusiastic about it, you know? I remember one woman I convinced to join; she was a widow with two daughters and she agreed because, she said, 'this way my daughters won't have to work as servants for the whites.' There were about fifty Cubans in the movement in Cueto. I still remember Linda, Yeya, La China, Aurela, a teacher called Victoriana Ochoa and Sibí, a Jamaican called Miss Luz.

To raise funds to buy the boats we'd go in – we already had one, the 'Antonio Maceo'– we had to pay dues of twenty-five centavos a week, they held raffles and parties where they charged to get in and for everything on offer. The activity which made the most money was like a fair, where they sold traditional food and candies, Jamaican and Cuban; there weren't any alcoholic drinks, just natural fruit juices.

The parties were great fun, lots of people came. Of course, there weren't very many places where poor – and especially black – people could go to enjoy themselves. The music they played to liven up the atmosphere was from both countries; for this they had to reach an agreement: as the Cubans wanted their music and the Jamaicans wanted theirs, they decided to draw lots and play the music of the winners. And what a commotion from whoever won!

Black people couldn't be mayors or anything like that; black teachers got sent to work in Monte Ruth or Jarahueca, or somewhere like that out in the country. In town? Forget it! Not there. An important position would not be given to a black person even if they were capable. There were exceptions but only if it were advantageous to the politicians. The *negritas* were put to work in the houses of whites, where they'd have all their hair cut off 'so as not to have to see them with messy kinks.' Well, there were lots of things I didn't agree with and, although I felt myself to be very Cuban, that's why I wanted to go; though I had no idea where Africa was. I knew it existed, that it was one of the five continents, but I had no idea where it was. But I was sure things would be different there.

There was a Jamaican song that, roughly translated, went something like:

> *Run good man*
> *run good man*

run good man
steal a bit of rice and chicken
put it in your pockets ...

I don't remember all of it, I wouldn't be able to write it down; it wasn't in English, it was a language like in the calypsos.

There was such a lot of activity when they announced Garvey's visit to Cuba, that was around 1921 or so. There were parties more often to increase the collection of funds. We also had collective dinners and we all contributed money for expenses. We'd pay for everything we ate or drank and what was left over we gave to the treasurer. Charles Clark and another one whose name I can't remember gave speeches; we increased the visits to convince more people to go.

I couldn't go to Santiago when Garvey was there, I had to work, but the Jamaicans all went and – my goodness! – how happy they were when they came back to Cueto, such excitement and high hopes they brought back with them. They told us all the details of the visit. Going to Africa, to the home of our ancestors, living like a big family, all equal, that was true liberty. That was the message the Jamaicans brought.

The activities dwindled after a while. They persecuted the blacks who ran the organization, some of them were sent back to their country. Everything started to go a bit underground, they hardly collected any money anymore; I didn't really know what happened, why it fell apart,[12] but it was sad, very sad! All our hopes dashed. For me that was as if suddenly – bam! – someone punched me: I had to stay in Cuba, keep suffering because I was black. After that I was sure of one thing: I had to prevail over discrimination!

There's still a long way to go

Racial discrimination in Cuba was very intense and a complicated issue. Whites discriminated against blacks and these harboured resentment against whites; black people who had managed to gain a certain economic and social position, felt the same about poor blacks and even looked for a white woman to marry. But those were few, in comparison with the huge mass of blacks who achieved neither economic solvency nor any education.

There were associations for blacks, and for mulattos. Here in Santiago were 'Luz de Oriente' for mulattos and 'Aponte'[13] for blacks, both for people of a certain educational and economic level. For poor blacks, 'El Gran Casino Cubano'; but for the very poor, the illiterate, the great mass of black and mulatto people, for them there was nothing! Colour was also a problem when it came to getting an education. The majority of blacks who studied – who managed it – went to the School of Arts and Trades, or the Normal School for Teachers. Very few did their bachillerato,[14] because it was very difficult to carry on; the same happened with the School of Home and Commerce, it was very unusual for a black person to study there.

Now, you don't have to worry about the colour of your skin. Although, really, I do know of quite a few people who still have serious racial problems. I've heard of black girls who haven't got jobs in an office, in favour of white girls; positions not given to a black person with any old excuse in order to ensure a white person gets it. There are lots who still have that mentality; I don't know why they insist on keeping this problem alive.

I'm very observant and I've noticed there are not very many black actors and those few have never been protagonists of a novel or a story. They're always maids, dock workers, slaves, well, it depends on the plot. At the beginning of the revolution it made sense, we didn't have much knowledge, but now! – after all these years... Could it be that writers don't like to write novels with blacks as the protagonists or is it something else? To my way of seeing, those who keep alive the problems of discrimination do a lot of damage. In this sense, there's still a long way to go!

I like to read all kinds of things: the works of José Martí, books about the history of Cuba, works of world literature, books of poetry by different authors; but lately I've been reading everything that has been written or is being written about black people – though it's not much – but some of the things annoy me, I don't know, they don't go deep enough, they don't interview the old people, who were, after all, the ones who had to suffer that whole situation. I think as we die out the writers will get further from the truth. Because it's not just what it says on paper: papers will back up whatever's put down on them. Another thing is how each person who uses documents interprets them. I recognize the effort and the determination; but in the end, the books don't really reflect reality that well.

A black girl

When I was a little girl, I remember there was a time when I lived in La Maya with my mama – Isabel – and my brother, Pepe and my sister, María – the two lightest of all. Everything I did bothered Isabel. It seems I was in the habit of keeping my mouth open; this was the cause of great distress for her, so every time she saw me she'd shout: 'Reyita close your mouth before your *bemba*[15] hits your knees.' And I'd look in the mirror and it seemed to me I didn't have any such *bemba*, comparing my lips to other black people – some of whom did have very thick lips – I noticed that mine were quite thin, but, of course, not like my brother and sister's.

31

But my mother's complex made her see things. This was such a serious problem for her, when my sister María – who loved me very much – dressed me up in the afternoons and sent me out for a stroll with the other girls of the neighbourhood, if Isabel saw me, she'd call me over, give me a shake and say: 'Reyita, you're nobody's little clown to go along to be laughed at', and she'd take me straight to the house where she worked. Oh, goodness gracious! – how I suffered with that.

Once – when I was a bit older – there was a party in the neighbourhood; it was a birthday party for one of the neighbours, Iluminada, she was called. We were all excited about going and your aunt María dressed me up and did my hair and had me looking so pretty. The three of us went along. I was the only *negrita*. We went past the place where Isabel worked and she said to me:

– Reyita, where do you think you're going?

– We're going to Iluminada's birthday party.

– Reyita, you can't go play the fool among all the mulattos, come in here and wash the white folks' dishes!

Isabel was so embarrassed and, even though I was all dressed up, she wouldn't let me go because I was the only *negrita*; my other sisters certainly went. Not me because, although I wasn't an ugly girl, I was a black girl. Deep down Isabel wasn't really bad. For a long time I never understood her, but when I got old I realized that my poor mother was a victim of the misfortune we blacks all suffered, as much in previous centuries as in this one. I'll explain a few things about her that you don't know, and you'll see I'm right.

Isabel

When slavery was abolished and Tatica left the Hechavarría plantation together with Basilio, my mother's father – one of the owners – wouldn't let her take Isabel. He exerted his right

32

of paternity not to raise her, his daughter, like a señorita, but rather to keep her working as a maid, which was what she'd done almost since she learned to walk, in exchange for not much clothing and bad food.

Your grandmother gave birth to a baby boy in 1889, who they named Eduardito. This wasn't a child of love either, but the result of abuse by Isalgué, husband of one of the Hechavarría girls. To avoid a scandal they threw my mama, along with her son, out of the house. There was no compassion – just the opposite – they acted as if the shameless, brazen one had been my poor mother. Isabel was ashamed to go to her mama's house so she went to work cutting cane at a farm near La Maya.

Her life there was sheer martyrdom. She had no one to take care of the baby while she went on the harvest, so she took him with her; she'd lay him down under a sapling until break time, which she'd take advantage of to give him food and water. She lived like that for a few years, until she met Francisco Ferrer, a white man who worked in the Los Cedros sugar plant.

Francisco had means. He promised to take her with him, get her a house and take care of her and her son. He was married but, as you can imagine, her situation was so difficult she agreed to go with that man. He set her up in Los Cedros, in a little wooden house which must have seemed like a palace to my mama compared to the barracks where she'd been living. But she didn't stop working; she kept cutting cane to have her own source of money.

She had two children by that man: José, who was called Pepe, in 1892, and María, in 1894. These children of your grandmother's were '*adelantados*'[16] : Pepe and María's skin was almost white, they had fine, not very curly hair, and their features, also very fine, had nothing in common with mine.

When the war of '95 broke out, Francisco didn't want to suffer the uncertainties of that struggle and he went to Santo Domingo. Your grandmother, along with her three small children joined up with the families of the *Mambí*.[17] They went from place to place, encountering all sorts of vicissitudes; her oldest child, Eduardito, helped her with the younger ones until he died of smallpox. My poor mother had to dig a grave with her bare hands, wrap her son in palm leaves and bury him; but she couldn't allow herself the luxury of faltering. She still had Pepe and María and she had to look out for them.

On one occasion a *Mambí* column camped where she was staying. One of the soldiers liked my mama and tried to help her as much as he could. He and Isabel became husband and wife. She followed the column wherever they went, along with the other *Mambí* families. That soldier was my father, Carlos Castillo Duharte, the only black man Isabel would ever share her life with. During the rest of the war, she had three more children: Candita, Evaristo and Nemesio.

One time, the *Mambí* families were hiding down in a dry riverbed, because a column of Spaniards was about to pass by, but Candita was crying and crying because she was very ill. The rest of the women, afraid of being caught, said to your grandmother: 'Isabel, find a way to make that child be quiet.' Not knowing what to do, she left the other children and walked and walked until she came to a little stream.

She was carrying her daughter pressed against her chest. When the little girl stopped crying Isabel realized she was dead. Once again she had to dig a grave with her bare hands and bury her child wrapped in leaves. She couldn't stop to cry or mourn, she would run the risk of the group moving from where they were and not being able to find the rest of her children. Evaristo and Nemesio didn't survive either. Laden with shortages and calamities, she reached the end of the war with my brother Pepe and my sister María. Isabel went to 'El Desengaño' with her children and Mamacita, my paternal grandmother.

After a while she and my dad decided to start a little diner in La Maya; they struggled to get by. During this time my brother Julián was born. Despite the effort they put in, the restaurant went bankrupt, so they had no alternative but to go back to 'El Desengaño', and that's when I was born. Back then my dad was impossible. According to Isabel, he was a terrible womaniser and she got tired of putting up with it. Since he didn't look after her properly, she decided to leave him. She left Julián with Mamacita, took Pepe and María to live with a cousin she had in La Maya, and went with me to Guantánamo.

She got lodgings in the barracks of the 'Soledad' sugar plant and went to work cutting cane. There were some Haitians living there. During the harvest she left me with an old woman, who was the only one who stayed in the barracks. I only have very vague memories of that time but I could never forget Cherisse, a Haitian who, when she didn't have to work, would piggyback me around the forecourt! Once she started a fight with me on her back, but you know, I don't remember receiving a single blow.

One of the administrators of the plant was attracted to your grandmother and he made her all sorts of promises which she believed. Result: she got pregnant again. That man was called Agustín Rodríguez, he made her a little wooden house and we lived there until we went to 'La Dolorita', a property belonging to my aunt Casilda – my grandmother Tatica's sister – , where she went to give birth, and where she left me while she went off with the new-born, your aunt Gloria. She didn't go back to Guantánamo, because she realized that Agustín wasn't going to solve any of her problems.

Aunt Casilda had a son by her former owner and he *had* been recognized by his father and studied law in France. When my mama went to have her baby at the farm, he was there. Poor man! For defending peasants, and especially blacks, he disappeared: one day he went out and didn't come back, they never heard another word about him, not what happened nor what his destiny was. They disappeared him, it was not in their interest to have an educated black man around.

I can't really remember what my life was like in Aunt Casilda's house, around 1906. All that's clear in my mind is that she lived alone and she had to go out to work the land and take care of her animals. When she left in the mornings she'd tie me to one of the table-legs, she'd leave a container of water and another of food. There, I'd relieve myself, I'd sleep, wake up, until she came back in the afternoon, my goodness…! Then she'd untie me, wash me, feed me and let me wander around the house until it was time for bed. My aunt loved me very much, but there was nothing else she could do; it was the struggle to survive which obliged her to do that, she had to work for her livelihood and mine.

I'm sure mine was not the only case, there were worse out in the country, the thing is, nothing is ever written about this. It seems writers aren't interested in this or they don't know about it. My life went along like that until one day your grandmother came to get me. We were going to live with dad again in another bit of wilderness.

His sister had given him a little piece of land in a place called 'Los Caguairanes' – near Cuatro Caminos – where he built a house of *yagua* and *guano*,[18] and he convinced your grandmother he'd changed. She believed him and they got together again. Your aunt María and I went with them. Gloria had gone to Guantánamo with her dad – Agustín – because he hadn't any children with his wife.

It was the start of a new life, preparing the soil for planting, raising animals. You have no idea what it was like, living in the middle of the bush, no neighbours, no electricity, getting water from the river, collecting firewood. Because for poor people – and especially the very poor – their children could never be children, let alone play; their game was to work almost from the time they learned to walk. We threw ourselves into putting that place in working order, even if it were for just enough to survive.

When my mama was happiest, your grandfather went off to work far away in the 'El Cuero' mines, and he didn't come back. This was a problem for poor women, especially poor black women: their husbands would go off far away to find work, to improve the economic situation, and in the majority of cases wouldn't come back. My mama, María and I worked till we dropped and we got by. What a huge effort we had to make to keep going, attend the crops and the few animals we had, and to top it off, she was pregnant again. But your grandmother had no luck: when my dad left, his sister took back the little piece of land.

I remember the day we left... The road, the bundles of what little clothing we had, a goat and on the way, a new member of the family: José María, 'Cuto', my youngest brother. With nowhere to go, we returned to 'El Desengaño'. Mamacita welcomed us with affection and fondness, but Isabel had her pride, she felt she couldn't live there when she was no longer with your grandfather. After a while we went to La Maya, to the house where your uncle Pepe lived. Mama started working at whatever she could.

If you only knew how naughty I used to be! One day, mama was in the yard doing someone's washing and when it finished boiling she put on an *ajiaco*[19] for the evening meal. She made her a*jiaco* with pork, vegetables, lots of vegetables: *malanga,*[20] potatoes, squash, yams and sweet corn. There was a little cat in the house and I said to myself: 'I'm going to put him in the *ajiaco* so it'll have more meat.' I grabbed him, took the lid off the pot, threw him in and put the lid back on. My God! When your grandmother went to dish it out and realized I had not only ruined the food, but killed the cat as well, she nearly killed

37

me too, I didn't do it to be bad, I just wanted to add to the meal. Imagine! I was about six or seven then. You didn't need to be much older to be put to work in some well-to-do whites' house.

Later she met Narciso Barrientos – a mulatto mule-driver – who had a little house in a place called Belleza. He fell in love with her and asked her to take him as her husband. After about three or four months she went to live with him. Your uncle Cuto, my grandmother Tatica and I went there with her. Barrientos had a daughter called Agustinita who lived there too, and who was more or less the same age as me. That house was in the middle of the bush, we had no neighbours, which made it even gloomier, to which must be added that man's extremely difficult character. Agustinita and I wanted to move to town because we hated the darkness.

Once we threw a burning ember on the thatch roof, intending to burn down the house so we'd have to move away from there. Well, I don't know – I don't remember exactly what happened – they put the fire out, but what happened next you can't possibly imagine: what a terrible beating we got! They practically set us on fire, too, like we'd done to the house. In the end, only part of the roof burnt, because the river was nearby, just there, and they were able to soak the roof and prevent the fire from spreading.

On that farm we all had to work very hard and Agustinita and I had to sort plantains. When Barrientos arrived with the panniers full, we separated the big plantains from the medium and small ones, because when he packed them he put big ones underneath, then little ones, then big ones on top. When he offered them for sale in town, they'd see the big ones on the top and when he emptied them, the big ones on the bottom. And he'd earn a few *quilos*[21] more. He sold the medium ones separately. Agustinita and I naturally wanted nothing to do with plantains, what we were interested in was playing. Our only pleasure was to swim in the river, hunt for crayfish and eat guavas – there was an enormous guava grove there. Those were the only entertainments we had.

One day, your uncle Pepe came to visit; and he made us a little play-house of *yaguas* and *guano* in the yard. Whenever we could we'd escape into our dream world for a few moments, never for long, we had to sweep the whole yard in front of the house, fetch water from the river, gather firewood for the kitchen and get the corn off the cobs for the animals, and if Barrientos decided to check up on us and surprised us playing, what a thrashing!

He mistreated us badly. My grandmother defended us but my mama didn't; she flattered him and always took his side. I think she wanted to maintain the stability and security she had there, because it was hard but less so than constantly moving from place to place.

After a while Juan, my father's brother – who didn't have any children – came to see me and asked my mama if she'd let me go live with him. Isabel agreed and after three or four days we left. I'll never forget poor Agustinita screaming for them to let her go with me, to not leave her alone. I can still remember her voice shouting:

– Adiós, Reyitaaa!

– Adiós, Agustinitaaa! – over and over again until our voices were lost in the distance. It never occurred to me I'd never see her again. From then on, I never again lived with my mother. She could relax her complexes about me.

Isabel separated from Barrientos and went back to La Maya. She had her last child there, María de la Cruz. Your aunt Gloria's father was widowed and, since he had no one to look after the little girl, he brought her back to your grandmother, who went back to Santiago and got a job as a servant. By this time, Pepe and María were married. Your aunt María was widowed after ten years of marriage. She had two sons. Her husband's family played a dirty trick – they were never in favour of the marriage because she was mestizo. From the inheritance she was supposed to receive, they only bought her a little house in Santiago and gave her seven hundred pesos. That was quite a sum in those days, so you can just imagine how much money that man must have had!

Gloria's dad bought her a house too, beside María's. Your grandma and your aunt María de la Cruz – 'Cusa' – and Cuto went to live with her. María sewed in a factory, Gloria got a job as a conductor on a bus and they started to make new friends – almost all white. Your grandmother got her wish for stability and completely changed her way of life; she always dressed in white and María made her clothes. Like a good Catholic, she went to mass every Sunday.

Despite how well she began to live, Isabel continued to have that complex between her almost white, mulatto and black children. So she set herself up in the extension of Gloria's house and even cooked separately, so when her black children and grandchildren came to visit they wouldn't interfere with the life of the lighter-skinned part of the family. Gloria and María suffered terribly with that problem. But your grandmother thought and acted like that... nothing was going to make her change. It was the result of racial discrimination.

Those prejudices made your grandmother sacrifice even her own tastes to maintain an appearance, I never could understood it. Just imagine! She loved the *tumba francesa*,[22] but she never went, so no one would see her. When she was old – when they danced *tumbas* in the carnival as if they were a *comparsa*[23] – she'd come to my house and tell my sons, Monín or Nené, to come out with her to *arrollar*.[24] On the way back she'd ask the boys not to tell anyone. Why did she have to do it secretly? Why live attached to prejudices? Only we knew she liked the *tumba francesa*.

A woman without prejudices

One woman who did live without complexes and had no interest in improving the race – as folks used to say back then – was my grandma, Mamacita. She was average height, pretty, with a very good figure, a tiny waist and broad hips. They say – because I didn't notice these things – that her best features were her legs and her bosom. She liked to wear long housedresses, mostly white ones; she also wore full skirts and short blouses. The shoes she wore were something like slippers. She didn't like 'dangly things' – as she used to say. She had a gold chain, gold bracelets and rings, I never saw her wear any other jewellery.

Her name was Emiliana Duharte, daughter of Caridad Muchulí and Vicente Duharte. Mamacita married Antonino Castillo – my paternal grandfather – a free black bricklayer, and they went to live in a little house where Martí and Calvario streets are today, here in Santiago. My great-grandmother was not in favour of this marriage, she felt Mamacita would 'put back the race'. Blacks, and especially older blacks, always considered it important to marry white, because the lighter your skin the fewer vicissitudes of discrimination you'd have to undergo. I can understand my great-grandmother's preoccupations having suffered greatly for being black.

Antonino and Mamacita had seven children: six boys and a girl. The youngest was my dad, who coincidentally was born on the 10th of October 1868, the first day of the Ten Year War. My grandfather joined up and was killed. My grandmother, who had followed him into the resistance, returned to Santiago after the Zanjón Pact.[25] From that moment on she had to struggle to survive, to feed and shelter herself and her children. Mamacita had a very strong character and ensured that each of her children learned a trade. She made candies to sell from the house and in the streets; she'd also put out a table on festival days in Santiago and the surrounding villages. On one occasion, at the festival of San José – patron saint of La Maya – where she'd gone, as usual, to sell her wares, she met Francisco Mondeja, a white man known as Pancho, owner of 'El Desengaño', a farm in that village.

There were several Mondeja brothers. Papá Panchito – as we all called him – never married Mamacita, but they lived together for thirty-seven years, until she died. Their union was a scandal; his family felt dishonoured, but he cared more for Mamacita. When the War of 1895 began, all the Mondejas went to the island of Jamaica. Mamacita didn't want to go with Papá Panchito and she joined the insurrection with all her children. Lucas and Mateo were taken prisoner and sent to the prison camp at Ceuta,[26] where they died; the rest survived. Uncle Vicente was a captain; dad was a colour-sergeant; and the rest were soldiers. She and my aunt helped with whatever needed doing. When the war ended they went back to 'El Desengaño' and her sons started marrying and leaving the farm. She couldn't run it all on her own so she went to work in La Maya with my dad and mama. Your uncle Pepe and aunt María lived with them.

The Mondejas came back after the inauguration of President Estrada Palma[27] in 1902. Papá Panchito went to look for Mamacita in La Maya, but she'd already gone back to 'El Desengaño'; they got together again there. After a while he was given an important job with the 'Yunai'[28] – the United Fruit Company – in Banes and he took Mamacita with him. Your uncle Julián – who always lived with her – went too, escaping my mama's racial prejudices. I'll never forget Mamacita. Oh, my dear! If only I could have always lived with her, how different my life would have been! I wouldn't have suffered so much vexation and abuse and, especially, I wouldn't have been shunted about so much, from one relative's house to another.

42

Reyita, *la cagona!*[29]

The biggest humiliation of my life happened in La Maya, after my uncle Juan took me to live in his house with his wife Margarita Planas, Doña Mangá. This was around 1910. She was a very strong-willed woman, very strict and hard-working. Mangá had a goddaughter named Francisca, who they called Paquita. That was who she wanted in her house, but my uncle didn't. In spite of which, Paquita spent the whole day there and only went home at night.

They sent us both to a little school,[30] where we'd spend the mornings; in the afternoons we'd help with the housework. Paquita was bad, very bad! She wanted me to be thrown out of the house so she could inherit the shop my uncle had. You'll think a little girl of nine or ten years of age isn't going to know anything about things like that... but in those days, poverty, the struggle to make a living and just for subsistence made people mature very quickly, to which you have to add the suggestions of parents and grandparents. That ambition was what made Paquita so diabolical.

She misbehaved at school and she'd be punished; then she'd make me come with her and when we got home she'd say I was the one who had been punished. Mangá would give me a spanking for that. I don't want to remember everything that little girl put me through – the list would be too long – but I will tell you about the most painful episode. When Paquita was in the house, as well as pinching the candies Mangá made to sell and blaming it on me, before she left, she'd defecate in some corner of the house and when she came back the next morning the first thing she'd say was:

– Godmother, don't you smell some nastiness?

– Yes, it must have been Reyita during the night.

Paquita would find it straight away and Mangá would give me a real walloping. One day Paquita defecated in the laundry basket for white clothes and, when my aunt found it, fed up with all that – because she believed it was me – she punished me, and in such a way! She made me kneel down on the sidewalk in front of the house with my arms outstretched in a cross, palms up, and she put some of the filth on each of my hands, so that everyone who went by would see me. The kids shouted: 'Reyita, *la cagona*!' I wanted to die of shame, and worst of all, I was innocent. I was saved from that mortification by Tirso – a young man who lived in the neighbourhood – who came by and saw me, picked me up, washed my hands, and confronted the Doña, which startled her because no one ever dared raise their voice to her. She didn't punish me any more that day.

When my uncle found out about it, he had a serious quarrel with Mangá and put himself on guard – because I had sworn myself innocent of all Paquita's slurs. One day he caught her pinching candies and he called Mangá. What a beating, God in heaven! But she faced up to Mangá and cursed God and her godmother. That time she was sent home for good and I was left in peace for a while. Since I wasn't bad, I didn't give her reasons to hit me.

I worked like a mule, since I had to clean the house, fetch water, wash the baking pans and, on top of that, they put a little table out in the main street for me to sell candies. One time when Mangá couldn't make them, they rented the oven to a man from El Cristo, who they called Pepe, so he and his brother could work. Since I was the one who always washed the pans, Mangá wanted me to keep doing it and them to pay me. But they didn't want to and what they agreed was that they'd keep supplying me with candies to sell at the little stall. I liked it there because I didn't have to be in the house; on top of that, I made a little bit of money to buy things without Mangá knowing. Imagine! I was to sell the candies at three for a *medio*[31] and I would give them two; for every fifteen centavos, I made five. That was money back then!

People bought from me for two reasons: first because I was the youngest hawker and they probably felt sorry for me; and secondly because they were amused by a slogan I made up that went something like: 'Buy my candies, to take home to your kiddies'. I want you to know that the slogan was a very important factor in selling merchandise; many times buyers would come over to a stall attracted by the vendor's cry. But I don't really remember mine, it was so long ago, so many years ago. Oh, I was so little! Lord, what a tragedy to be poor!

There was a time when Mangá was taking in washing and ironing from the owners of the Mancebo store – the biggest in La Maya. I remember them all: Lino, Santiago and Vicente Mancebo. She made me wash the socks and the snotty handkerchiefs. Oh, those white boys had such runny noses! I'd cry when I had to do the washing. So I'd get a stick and stir the handkerchiefs around in the water to get some of the mucus off, and then scrape them. But it wasn't just washing, I had to iron them and fold the socks one inside the other.

But the doña was bad! No matter how hard I worked, she'd beat me mercilessly for any little thing. Look! This twisted finger of mine, that was from a stick she hit me with one time. What did my uncle do faced with that situation and those abuses? He didn't know anything about it, I never told him anything, he was very good and very noble and I didn't want to cause problems for him with his wife. He was happy having me at his side, I could never have caused him to suffer. In the end, what would it have solved? He'd have taken me back to my mama and there it would be worse.

Mysteries

Ever since I was a little girl I've seen visions I couldn't understand. In 'Belleza' – near our house – on a piece of land like a little island at the edge of a stream, I saw a white woman wearing a long, white dress. She was very attractive and elegant. She caught my attention and, astonished, I called your grandmother:

– Isabel, look at that elegant woman over there!

– I don't see anything.

I insisted because I was looking at her at that very moment, and since she didn't see anything, she got annoyed.

– Ah, Reyita, you and your silliness! What's an elegant woman going to be doing walking around in the middle of nowhere? Get a move on! Go and do something.

Sad at what she'd said to me, I turned to look again, but the woman wasn't there anymore. But by coincidence, three days later, Eldemira died. Her father was Pepe Revilla, the owner of all the land around there. His daughter was an attractive, well-dressed and elegant woman.

When I was living with Mangá in La Maya, she once put me to bed wearing some pyjamas which had belonged to a niece of hers who'd died. I didn't want to wear them and I begged her not to put them on me but she paid me no mind. When I lay down, I swear on the most holy, I felt someone was in bed with me, I heard her breathing and, feeling behind me in the bed, it felt like I touched the spine of someone beside me. I started to shout and when my aunt came in and I told her, she said,

– Damn it, Reyita! You and your visions all the time! She was really angry.

That annoyance made her put me to sleep outside in the yard, as punishment. I wasn't scared, looking up at the sky and seeing the stars, it seemed like they were greeting me and

46

smiling. I saw how they formed figures and I was chatting with them. And, in that silent communion with the stars, I fell asleep. *Ay, muchacha!* When Mangá looked out and saw me sleeping, she took offence and shouted:

– Juan, come and look at this and then tell me if that *negrita* isn't bad! She's not afraid of the dark, look how peacefully she's sleeping.

And she sent me to sleep in the bed.

Another night I dreamt that from each leaf of the tamarind tree – the one in the vacant lot in front of the house – was hanging a number five, and in the dream I delighted in the way they swayed back and forth in the breeze. In the morning the lottery salesman went by and he had, among others, a strip with 5 555. I told Mangá and I said,

– Buy it, Mangá, maybe it'll win.

– Oh, listen to the little witch! Because you're going to be a witch. Look here, I'm not buying a thing.

The ticket seller, who didn't want to lose the opportunity of a sale, said:

– Buy it, doña! Don't underestimate the little girl's revelation.

Mangá, having been asked, bought one little section of the ticket, the lottery man tried to convince her to buy the whole strip, but she didn't want to. And when they announced the lottery on the following Saturday, the number had won the third prize. Mangá was so sorry not to have bought the whole strip and spent a few days sulking about it. I was glad she didn't win because she'd called me a witch but deep down I felt sorry because the lottery was one of the few hopes poor people had to make a little money and solve some of their problems.

Another time I was out playing in front of the house, and it got rather late. Mangá called me to come in and eat. When I was passing by the shop, I saw a young neighbour of ours called Miguel Angel – four or five years old – standing in front of

47

me with a bright blue halo around his head. I called him and he didn't answer and when I went closer to see what he had on his head, he disappeared. I ran home, scared, called Mangá and told her what had happened.

–Damn you and your visions, always seeing things! Go on, off you go, get to bed!

And she sent me to bed without any supper.

The next day in Miguel Angel's house they were doing the cleaning and left some medicine within the child's reach, without noticing. The little boy grabbed the bottle and drank it down: it was carbolic acid. He was very ill and when he started to go into convulsions, Antoñica and Félix Estrada – his mama and dad – picked him up and ran to Leopoldo Depeaux' chemists. The child died on the way.

Those things terrified me. I couldn't explain them, of course. The grown-ups said I had '*mediumship*', but I didn't know what that was either. What I can tell you is that I 'saw' many, many things.

Mercy! Mercy!

Mercy, mercy, fall on your knees, have mercy! That's what the mediums cried at the spiritual session I attended with my aunt Mangá, one day in May, I can't remember exactly which, in 1912. They were terribly frightened by a vision I had, or, I should say, that I made them believe I'd had, because I didn't see anything. I swear! All the mediums saw something in a glass of water on the table and I said I saw something too. Listen, I'm going to tell you how it happened.

My aunt went to a spiritual session and took me with her because she didn't have anyone to leave me with. There were a few mediums around a table, my aunt among them and me on a little bench beside her. There were lots of other women there. After the prayers and invocations, the mediums saw lots of

48

things in the glass of water. I didn't see anything and got annoyed, I wanted to see something and concentrated on looking at the glass. Eventually, I decided to tell them I saw something too, although it wasn't true. I whispered to my aunt:

– Doña Mangá, I see something in the glass.

– Shut up, Reyita! You and your silliness!

I kept insisting until one of the mediums said to my aunt:

– Mangá, you know Reyita's got mediumship. Let her say what she sees.

And they gave me the floor; I wasn't intimidated, they let me speak and so I did. With an air of maturity I said:

– I see a line of men, marching to the hills, carrying bundles on the ends of sticks and old shotguns on their shoulders.

All the women there began to beg for mercy and to cry: 'War, it's war!' The fact is, three or four days later, many men with bundles over their shoulders went off to rise in rebellion, leaving from the yard in front of the house.

Many people gathered in my uncle's house. They'd get me to stand guard at the door; they'd shut themselves into the little room off the patio where they kept the things for making candies. One day several men came, among them Pedro Ivonet[32] and Evaristo Estenoz.[33] When my aunt Mangá went to greet them, Estenoz put his arm around me and kissed me. Ivonet too; Estenoz was very handsome. There was another one, another handsome black man – I can't remember his name – who made speeches; he spoke beautifully.

Back then I didn't know how important they were in the movement. They were the leaders of the Independent Coloured Party;[34] but I had heard that a senator called Morúa Delgado[35] had voted in a law against the creation of political parties for blacks, or rather, for people of only one race. 'Coloured' people considered this law unjust, because they realized they needed a political organization that would allow them to look for their own solutions to problems, because the white ones weren't helping at all.

Once the blacks were acquainted with the situation and in the best position to fight for their Party and their interests, Estenoz met with the President of the Republic, who said he'd support them in gaining this right, that they should pretend to take up arms against the government so he could get the Assembly and the Senate to believe there would be war between blacks and whites and to avoid it they must vote down the Morúa law, and thus the Party would be approved.

José Miguel's[36] real interest lay in securing the black vote, because he wanted to be re-elected President. When he couldn't achieve anything, he sent a commission into the hills with a message for the blacks: 'Don't surrender, I'll keep trying to solve the problem.' And to prevent them finding out what he'd promised the blacks, what he did was send the army under General Monteagudo[37] against them.

Just imagine! How were they to defend themselves? With old shotguns? With machetes? Since they didn't have enough weapons – and moreover they weren't intending to wage war – they were hunted down and captured. Poor souls! I saw them when they brought them down from the hills, tied up. They killed them, threw them in pits and set them on fire. Many of those who surrendered were taken to a place called Arroyo Blanco and there they were murdered by a group under the command of José de la Cruz Puente. They also killed my uncle Juan. Those are things you don't forget easily.

I remember the 30th of May. I woke up screaming, for when I opened my eyes I saw two animals that looked like geese at the bottom of my bed, shining as if they were alight; I was scared and started to shout and call my aunt. She got up angrily, well, she was very distressed by the death of my uncle Juan and the way things were going. When she asked me what was wrong, I said: 'Doña Mangá, look at those flaming geese, be careful they don't burn you.'

Mangá started to fight with me and insult me because she didn't see anything; she made me go back to bed and she went to her room. A short while later there was a knock at the street door and someone shouted: 'Doña Mangá, fire! fire! fire! The town's on fire!' Mangá grabbed her image of Santa Clara and went out to the yard praying and weeping. Meanwhile, Enrique Salcedo – a man who was living in the little store room where they kept the things for making candies – and I took the things out of the house. Salcedo, afraid he'd be taken prisoner, disguised himself as a woman, he put on one of Mangá's dresses and a scarf over his head.

The next day, Mangá was resting in what was left of the shop and Sergeant Baluja passed by and made a sign to her, meaning he was going to cut off her head. We had to flee from La Maya. We went to Banes, to Mamacita's house, but about six days later, due to the denunciation of a man called Pablo Correoso – who was the only one who knew where my aunt had gone – the Rural Guard showed up and arrested her. They accused her, along with other women, of having looted the town's main store. They said she was in the middle of the fire putting on perfume and shouting: 'Down with the Morúa law!' This was a lie, it was the pretext they used to arrest her, which they did because she was President of the Committee of Ladies for the Independent Coloured Party.

There were many arrests. Mario García Menocal,[38] candidate for the presidency of the Republic, took advantage of the situation. He demanded an amnesty for the black prisoners, but don't you go thinking he did it for justice nor anything of the kind: it was with the condition that when they were released, they and all their relatives voted for him. And that's how it was. He won the election, shameless rascal.

Mangá was sentenced to six months in prison. My poor aunt! That caused me great pain and tremendous indignation, because it wasn't fair, yet another injustice against black people. ... Margarita Planas, Doña Mangá, was a woman of very strong character, a great woman, but she wasn't fond of me.

During that time no one cared about the truth. But what strikes me is that after the triumph of the revolution it didn't occur to anyone to interview the people who lived through all that, those who lost family members, those who knew first hand the reasons for the formation of the Party. They should have done it, I don't think any of them are still alive. Now, I wonder, why haven't the historians gone into the details of what happened? It's very likely that the Americans were even involved. The result was that Cuba was left more divided than ever: whites on one side and blacks on another. Black people felt hatred and rancour for the whites and they humiliated and harassed the blacks. And that's how it was for a long time.

They called him Venus

In Banes I knew Fulgencio Batista,[39] who lived with his family quite close to my house, and who later became President of the Republic. At first I didn't know his name was Fulgencio, because everyone called him Venus. He had two brothers; one they called Panchín, the other's name was Hermelino. They were older – I was no more than ten – so I didn't see them much. They worked as *narigoneros*[40] or *quimbuerleros*[41] for the 'Yunai'. Batista and his brothers didn't live with their dad. Carmela was their mother, her husband was called Belisario. They'd come to my house to fetch water. Don Beli – as they called him – was always scolding Fulgencio: 'Venus, you'll get the back of my hand if you don't stop fooling around.' Because he'd hang about and take his time getting the water.

Don Belisario had a little shop where he sold fruit and vegetables; but it was a front for a clandestine store where they sold everything, very surreptitiously, because the Company wouldn't allow any businesses other than their own to operate in their territory. The Company store was daylight robbery. The workers were always in debt and, since they couldn't pay it off, they couldn't leave. They had to keep working, whether they wanted to or not, against their will. What a racket!

The '*Yunai*' was a very powerful company, with a lot of land devoted to cane and fruit crops. Along with their sugar and molasses production, they had cattle, horses, mules, and all kinds of animals. They had trains and ships, too. But how they exploited people, even children, because everyone had to work there. And still, they lived in terrible poverty. The '*Yunai*' workers weren't only Cubans, there were Jamaicans and Haitians too.

Batista was a happy, cheerful boy; he always wore shorts made of flour sacks, because Doña Carmela said that since he spent his whole time playing around he always ripped his clothes and life was hard enough as it was. He went to school at night, at the house of a woman named Caridad Reyes. Yes, her, the very one, to whom he gave a house when he made himself President. It was Papá Panchito who got him a job on the Company's railway, where he earned twenty centavos a day.

Outside '*Yunai*' territory there was a general store belonging to Emilio Galicia. Batista and my cousin Luis – who lived in Mamacita's house – stole a gold watch and some money from him. I don't know what they did with the watch but they hid the money behind one of the *yaguas* that lined the walls of Venus' house, and when Galicia accused them, they left town. Batista changed his name from Fulgencio and called himself Rubén. You see how strange life is – that turned out to be the name of the first martyr of his dictatorship, Rubén Batista.

He was very unscrupulous. When he became President, he ordered the construction of a big clock at the entrance to La Güira and went to inaugurate it personally, showing off his power and how he mocked justice. To top it all off, Batista invented some Indian ancestors for himself: he didn't want to acknowledge his black ones even being President of the Republic. As a little girl, I liked him very much; he was my friend. But when he got into power I never accepted the barbarities he committed, especially after the coup d'état of 10 March 1952.

I was happy during the time I lived in Banes, very happy. Mamacita liked to see me pretty and dressed-up. I had beautiful, long hair, and since she suffered from rheumatism and her fingers always ached, she'd pay to have my hair done and they'd tie it up with lovely big bows. I was always very smart. All my memories of Mamacita are good ones; she only ever beat me once, because I did something without asking permission, and I deserved the thrashing she gave me.

She had made me a rag doll, and I wanted to baptise it. I took the *libreta*⁴² and, behind Mamacita's back, bought all kinds of things: drinks, sweets, candies. I held the christening party in the courtyard of the house with all my little friends who I'd invited. There we were singing and having fun. When Mamacita heard all that and came to see, she said, 'Reyita, what's going on?' I didn't say anything. She shrugged her shoulders and looked very serious but she didn't insist, she didn't shame me in front of my friends. But after the *fiesta* had ended and everyone had gone, that's when my *fiesta* started! That was serious, goodness gracious, that was very serious!

Mamacita died in 1917 and I had to take charge of the house. There were thirteen men to look after. Papá Panchito was old, it was very hard work for me all by myself, and after my grandmother died things weren't the same. Papá Panchito died a few months later. A little while after that I left for Cueto, to look for my dad.

He lived with a woman with three children: two girls and a boy. They were around my age but real pests and rude. That woman was depraved; she liked telling dirty stories in a loud voice and talked about awful things with her friends. My dad worked in a bakery and didn't earn much, so she took in washing and ironing to help. When I arrived, being another mouth to feed, she made me wash and iron with her. And her kids just lazed around! I did not like that woman.

The schoolteacher of Báguanos

In Cueto I went to work in the house of Señor Gaston Gayol and his wife Pradina. I took care of their children, gave them classes, looked after them, told them stories, took them for walks. Señor Gayol, noticing my interest, said, 'There are no teachers in Báguanos; there aren't any teachers anywhere along that way yet, and it would be a good idea for Reyita to have a school so she could have more pupils.' They took me to Báguanos and I set up the little school in a private house. When they saw it was working and saw their children progressing, they decided to put up a big structure without walls, with a wooden roof and floor. They made a blackboard and I bought a map of the world and a bell. They called it '*La escuelita*'. I eventually had sixty-two students.

I had no great knowledge, but I had the ability to teach what I knew. I bought some books – more like primers – that were called *Epítome*. There were some on Geography, some on Arithmetic, Grammar, Physiology. They were question and answer books. For example: 'Who discovered America and why is it so named? America was discovered by Christopher Columbus…' And so on and so on; the questions and then the answers. Like, for example: 'The human body consists of how many sections? The human body consists of three sections: the head, the trunk and the extremities.' I studied them at night and during the day I taught them to the kids. The parents said, 'Look how much she knows, that *negrita!*', and word got round and everyone sent their children to my little school. I taught them the hymns, I marched them around, we played *rueda de caracol;* [43] in short, it was just like a real school. They gave me presents, I had more than enough things.

The families of the few black pupils in my little school couldn't afford the monthly fee, and I didn't charge them when I saw their eagerness to learn. I felt like an important person. I was the village schoolteacher! The children loved me and their parents respected me.

From the money I made from the Báguanos school, I handed some of it over to Señor Gayol, and with the rest I bought myself a few luxuries, mostly clothing. I saved some of it, too, I had to think of the future. I was fifteen then.

But 'happiness is short-lived for the poor' as the Cuban saying goes. When they established the public school there, the sea swept away my sand-castle. Where to go? I had no choice but to go to Santiago de Cuba; leaving behind those two years in which I had been so happy. The very day of my departure, as I was leaving the village, the siren started up to announce the opening of the *Central.* [44]

Telling you about all that reminds me of a time, when I lived in Barracones many, many years after I'd left Báguanos, that I was going down the street and I heard 'Señorita, señorita' and when I looked round there was a man who said, 'You don't remember me, do you?' It was one of the students from that little school. He was an electrician and he lived and worked here. I felt so happy that he remembered me! That was a prize. That was my teaching 'certificate'.

A huge success

I lived in the house of my cousin, Carmen Duharte. She took in bed linen to wash for the Hotel Imperial; I had to iron the sheets that she washed and she paid me one peso. What an abuse! Ironing twenty-one sheets for one peso! Her daughter, Emelina, had a tutor who came to give her classes to prepare her for the *bachillerato* entrance exam. I was desperate to learn and to make something of myself so I put the ironing board close to where they had the classes. When the teacher arrived, I'd let the stove go out so it looked like I wasn't ironing because I was waiting for the coal to light – in those days irons were actually made out of iron and heated with coal – so I could eavesdrop on the classes.

I caught everything he said, and I would furtively write down any word I didn't understand, and look it later up in the dictionary. At night, when everyone went to sleep, I'd take Emelina's books and study by the light of a kerosene lamp. So that's how it went, and when the day came for Cecilio Serret – that was the tutor's name – to give Emelina a test, she didn't know the answers to a lot of questions. I felt sorry for her and tried to whisper the answers to her. Some she heard and answered, others she didn't. The tutor noticed and said, 'How is it that you're prompting her when I teach Emelina, not you, and you're always over there ironing? I'm going to give you a test to see if you've picked up the material I've been teaching Emelina.' He gave me the test and I passed.

Professor Serret went through all the formalities so I could be admitted to the Institute, because he said it would be a shame if someone so intelligent couldn't study. We both passed. You had to wear patent leather shoes, linen stockings, a yellow gabardine skirt and a little hat. I couldn't buy them; what I earned ironing wasn't enough. In the end I never enrolled – without a uniform, you couldn't go! I begged Carmen Duharte to lend me the money, that I'd work at whatever I could in my spare time to pay her back, but she wouldn't. I asked other relatives, but they only ended up saying: 'That *negrita* has gone crazy.'

Naturally, my mother found out about it and she was not only completely indifferent but joined in with the gossip. I didn't feel crushed, no. I had succeeded! It was wonderful knowing I could do it, even if it didn't work out. I was very sad, but I soon recovered: I was young, I could take another route. I'd just turned eighteen.

Chapter 2

Remembering is a voyage,
returning
to the village where something more
than time passed

Why I married a white man

I had, and still do have, a lot of faith in the Virgin of Charity
of El Cobre.[45] One day I knelt down clutching her image and
asked her for a good, hard-working, white husband, without a
family that would be ashamed of me for being black. I know
you understand why I wanted to marry a white man. It goes
without saying, now, that I love my race, that I'm proud to be
black, but in those days, marrying white was vital. The
Virgencita granted me a handsome, young, hard-working, good-
looking man. He had many virtues, he wasn't a carouser, a
drinker, or a womanizer. In return for this request, I promised
the Virgin to put her image – in the house I'd have when I got
married – in front of the main street door so everyone would
see her.

When I went back to Cueto in 1920, I made my living
with a little school I set up in the house; in the mornings I had
a dozen kids and in the afternoons I gave classes to the children
of the owners of the Cuba y España Hotel – Miguel Muñoz
and Manuel Carderrosa. They became very fond of me. After a
while, they needed a waitress at the hotel and they offered it to
me.

I went to work there and lived there, too. I got along well with the owners and, since I worked hard, had no problems. I was very sociable and agreeable. I laughed at everything and I was never in a bad mood, moreover, I was always singing. There was a man who came every evening to play in the billiards room downstairs in the hotel. Every time I went up or came down the stairs, he tilted his head up to look at me. This used to make my blood boil! It really enraged me, I was fed up with him doing that.

His name was Antonio Amador Rubiera Gómez, he was twenty-eight years old and worked as a telegraph operator for the railway company *Welfargo*. Tired of that, one day when he looked up at me, I said:

– If you want to look, look!

And I lifted up my dress. In those days we wore bloomers, petticoats, slips and bodices.

And when I did that, he came running up the stairs behind me, grabbed me and covered me in kisses, at first it bothered me:

– If you don't let me go I'll scream – I said. But he paid no attention and kept kissing me. My goodness! He made me feel something, you know?

– Kiss me!

I kissed him.

– So, does this mean you love me and we're a couple now?

At first I wouldn't agree, but he kept on insisting. I had these beautiful, long ponytails, and he'd say:

– Look what gorgeous hair you have! Let's see you smile.

– I don't feel like smiling.

He'd keep on till he made me laugh.

– What a beautiful smile!

And so on and so on, until I realized I loved him. Since I lived in the hotel, he spoke to the owners to arrange the

60

wedding, and after a few months we were married. They arranged a big hall, flowers, cakes, drinks, they brought in the notary; in short, we got married. It was a simple affair, but very significant for me. I glimpsed security, the home I'd never had, without anyone discriminating against me or being ashamed of the colour of my skin or my lips or my nose; at last, I was heading for bliss. Did your grandmother come to the wedding? I didn't bother to let her know. There was no one there from my family. Why? I was betting on my future, my destiny; I'd tell them in good time. This was in 1923.

Since Rubiera was white and didn't hesitate in marrying me, when he suggested we go to Cárdenas to meet his family I figured they'd be of the same mind-set. His dad's name was Rufino, he was Asturian, from Gijón, in the province of Oviedo, and his mama was Dominican,[46] daughter of an Asturian, also from Gijón, her name was Carlota; he only had one sister.[47] I didn't get to know them.

When that Señora[48] opened the door, he said:

– Mama, this is my wife!

– What? A black woman! Not in my house!

And she slammed the door in our faces.

I felt so ashamed and humiliated that I ran off. Rubiera caught up with me at the next corner, tried to explain, but there was no explanation, so I decided to return immediately to my house.

– You can keep your family!

– Reyita, I'm really embarrassed by my mother's attitude, but I swear she'll never have the opportunity to humiliate you again. They're as good as dead for me, I'll never come back to this house.

And he never did. He didn't even go to Cárdenas when his parents died. He returned when you were all grown-up and you made him go to his sister, María Julia's, death-bed.[49]

61

When we got back to Cueto my new life began. I had a house, a husband, and I felt secure. I went to Santiago with Rubiera to introduce him to my mama and my brothers and sisters. Isabel was very pleased, in the first place, because he was white and her grandchildren weren't going to be dark black; she congratulated me for having understood the importance of improving the race and, secondly, because my life would become stable.

Mistress of what? Simply Reyita!

In Cueto, where I lived for seven years, I had a little wooden house with a zinc roof and a big window looking out front onto a little garden where I planted roses. I've always liked flowers, so ever since I've had my own house, I've always grown them; they give me a lot of pleasure. I also had a nice set of wicker furniture and even a phonograph. On my first birthday as a married woman Rubiera gave me a white Manila shawl, because our financial situation was quite comfortable. My first two children were born in that house. Rubiera always said,

– I want a dozen children, a big family.

– *Ay, viejo!*[50] Don't you think that's too many?

– No, Mima, I want twelve children.

I never did anything to prevent them. My children are all two years apart because while I was breast feeding I didn't get my period. Tata is three years older than Monín because she didn't take to solid food and kept breast feeding all that time.

After my first child was born, a white neighbour came to see me and I was struck by the emphasis when she said:

– Oh, look how dark the child is!

And they say black children are born light and sometimes half white.

The same day that white woman came to see me, but in the afternoon, came Marcelina, who was an older woman. We got along really well. She was black, a servant in some white people's house. Almost everybody around there called each other Don or Doña[51] – Don José, Doña Amelia, Doña Caridad – and I noticed that with me they didn't use it, so I asked her:

– Marcelina, why is it when I'm a married woman and married to a white man, at that, they don't call me Doña?

She smiled at me sadly and said:

– Why are they going to call you Doña? These people get called Doña because they're white and rich; but you, *negra prieta*[52] – married to a white man, yes, but poor – mistress of what? Simply Reyita!

At the time I didn't really understand what she meant, I was very naïve; I did later, did I ever! Now I have lots of riches, not material but spiritual ones: my children and my grandchildren, how wonderful! They are teachers, doctors, engineers, professors, technicians and workers. No drunks or thieves. I feel rich, but even with such wealth I don't want anyone calling me Doña, I'd rather be Reyita, simply Reyita. Isn't that right? It's nicer.

What happened when Marcelina came to visit me didn't disturb my happiness. Time went by, now I had children growing up healthy and strong; when I brushed my little girls' hair I always remembered my mama. They had long, not very curly hair, too.

My neighbours – most of them white – discriminated against Rubiera for marrying me; and blacks, though they recognized that marrying a white man was 'a step forward', had certain suspicions, because Rubiera wasn't keen on me going off to other people's houses nor coming home to his full of people 'whispering', as he put it.

I never knew why we moved from Cueto to a wooden house with a dirt floor that Rubiera built in the pasture of a cattle farm near Marcané. They let him build it in exchange for us taking care of the animals, which I did with the kids – who were quite small – because he was still working on the railway. My furniture and almost all my things were ruined there. Rubiera was a bit rough at that time. Once I'd made a sponge cake to have for dessert and when I set the table I dished out a bowl of soup for each child – Pura and Chichí. They didn't want it, first they wanted dessert, your father told them:

– Eat your soup!

– We don't want soup, we want dessert.

– Eat your soup!

– No, we want dessert!

He got so angry that he took the whole sponge and threw it out the window. That really hurt! After I'd made it so lovingly.

I was pregnant and one day my friend Luisa came to see me – she had been my neighbour back in Cueto. When she saw what a state we were living in, she confronted Rubiera, because she didn't think I should give birth there. She had so much to say about it every time she came to see me that he decided to move us back to Cueto. To my great joy, we moved back to the same house we had before; your sister Tata was born there, we named her Antonia because I had her on your father's birthday. I don't know how our financial situation got so bad since Rubiera kept working in the same place.

Despite your father not causing me much worry over other women, there was one time I found out about one he had who was expecting a child. I'd heard it said that she was very poor and, within my means and with the help of my friend Luisa, we made up a basket for her. I asked the Virgin not to let another woman take my husband away. I asked fervently and from the heart. *Ay, muchacha!* That woman died – of thirst, they said – I don't really know. I don't know if the child survived, either. What I do know is, from that moment on, I have never asked the Virgin for anything that could possibly have fatal repercussions for someone; I've always lived with a guilt complex that that woman died because of what I asked.

With all the ups and downs in our fifty-four years of marriage, Rubiera and I stayed together until his death, in 1975.

Lend him to me, *Virgencita!*

Rubiera went to work in Bayamo because they tried to blame him for something he hadn't done; he was annoyed and got transferred. We lived in a humble house on General Capote street. My life wasn't much different to what it had been in Cueto: looking after my house and family; my fourth child was born there, Monín (Anselmo). The most important thing that happened to me was his illness: he was born weighing eleven pounds and at seven months he weighed eleven and a half pounds. He had dystrophy and another illness with a strange name.

Doctor Pedro Ramos was attending him and had prescribed a strict diet based on bacilli. Once he said it was unlikely the child could be saved and I was terribly upset. One day he woke up absolutely miserable and every time he saw someone eating he was driven to distraction. By noon there was no one who could quieten him, I didn't know what to do so I once again solicited the favours of my beloved *Virgencita*, I knelt down and said:

– Oh, my Virgin! Don't let my little son die. Save him for me! Lend him to me even if only till I see him become a man!

That night I had a dream and when I awoke I put it into practice: it was the answer – she gave it to me in this way. I got up and went to look for a small papaya, peeled it and cut it in four, threw one away, and put the rest to boil. I mixed the liquid with an equal quantity of milk and gave it to Monín.

He drank it down so greedily! When he finished he fainted and I thought he'd died and started to scream:

– I killed him, I killed him, I've killed my son!

The house filled with neighbours and one of them went to get Rubiera who arrived with the doctor. When Ramos examined the child he said he was alive and asked me what I'd given him. I explained and he said:

– In three hours give him the same again, if anything happens send for me, if not keep giving it to him and I'll be back tomorrow.

The child took to his milk very well and got better and better until he was out of danger and just marvellous.

The poverty that existed in Cuba – at that time – made poor people have a lot of faith in home remedies; that's why there were so many healers, or people like myself who, out of faith, tried to keep our families healthy with herbs and roots.

Before the story of the papaya water, the owners of a dairy came to see me – this was when they started pasteurising milk. They wanted me to lend them my skinny child, to take him around the city as an advertisement, lying in a cradle on a cart, to demonstrate that pasteurised milk was bad for them so people would keep buying fresh milk. Naturally, I not only said no, but insulted them as well and threw them out of my house. The last thing they said was:

– Señora, you're passing up an opportunity for money to feed your children.

Go to the devil! What you should be doing instead of spending money on advertisements is selling milk at affordable prices so poor children can be nourished and don't die of starvation. And not thinking so much about making yourselves rich!

That incident with Monín cost Rubiera his job, because he left work without asking permission or anything, so they fired him. His bosses had not one grain of humanity nor understanding: what did the health of a child of one of their workers matter to them? What interested them was that they worked, to make more money for the bosses.

Rubiera decided to change cities and we came here, to Santiago, to which I brought, along with his unemployment and my large family, my debt to the Virgin for Monín's life. When would she collect? And she did collect, but in such a way that I understood she always protected me.

We rented a little house in the Mariana de la Torre neighbourhood. The walls and floor were wooden, it was in the middle of a big vacant lot, had upstairs and down, two big windows looking out front and a zinc roof. Just imagine what life was like for us then: your dad out of work and five mouths to feed. I had to take in washing and ironing. What helped the most was the garden, but not right away.

I planted okra, corn, squash, yams and yucca in the land around the house. As well as feeding us, we sold some of the harvest to the neighbours, who were as poor as us. So, we just about managed. By that time Rubiera had got work as a driver of a garbage truck. He didn't earn very much, between the two of us we made just enough money to sustain the house and family.

What I never did was go and cry on my mother's shoulder, or to my brothers and sisters, either. They came to visit us once in a while. And when they did I'd take great pains to give the impression everything was going well. They weren't blind and if they didn't want to see, better for them not to see. After a while, the old man got a job as an office worker for *Expreso Velar*. We moved to a better house in the same development. My other four children were born there, you among them. From there we moved to a house across from the transport company where your dad worked. It was in Carlos Dubois street, better known as Barracones. We lived on the edge of the red light district. It didn't worry him, he was very proper and we were used to living inside the house.

Barracones

Barracones was a very picturesque street. It was narrow, the Santa Rita, Santa Rosa, and Santa Lucía ridges all met there. If you looked down the street you'd see the ocean, up the street, the tiled roofs and the balconies of the Santiago houses. There were many families in that neighbourhood who were poor but very decent. Barracones was like the main street for prostitutes. They always passed my house. You were always noticing them. I remember you asking me:

– Who are those women, all dressed up?

– They're workers in a noodle factory that's nearby.

– When I'm big I'm going to work in that factory.

I remember the vendors' cries from Barracones: 'Peanut brittle for bottles, trade em in; Broken necks or cracked lips, I'll trade…'

Or this other one: 'Hot tamales, spicy or mild, what'll it be…'

They struggled to survive, but it was a poor neighbourhood, so sometimes they got back home without a cent to buy something to eat.

I also remember those typical characters: Arbolito, a half-mad black man, tall, strong, always dressed in a black suit and a long overcoat – like the ones in movies called trench-coats – very dirty; long hair full of clumpy tangles. He retained, seemingly from his time of lucidity, a tremendous dignity in his way of standing and holding his head high. I haven't forgotten Cueco-duro either. She was a black woman of medium height and quite young, unhinged. Men took advantage of her dementia to have their way with her anywhere. She had several children. Cueco-duro was crazy, but she never allowed them to separate her from her children: she defended them like a lioness. Garrafón was another one; short, fat, Indian-looking, with long hair. They called him that because he had a hernia and his balls swayed from side to side when he walked. He sold belts which he hung over his shoulders and arms and also carried some in his hands. He wasn't very nice, he was always in a bad mood.

The most famous of all was… Not was but is, because he's still alive: el Diablo Rojo. What a character! Tall, thin, very nice, strong. He worked in advertising for various commercial products. He travelled all over Cuba on roller-skates. He taught dozens of Santiago kids how to roller skate. Everybody knows him. Now he's a crossing guard, on his roller skates, in front of a school in Trocha street, before school starts and when it gets out, because Diablo Rojo adores children.

Barracones had a very special musicality. The music from the jukeboxes, the drunks' rows, some women quarrelling with their children, their husbands, or a neighbour. The sound of the policeman's truncheon when he banged it on the lamppost. In short to live in Barracones was to live in a very special place.

The Plaza del Mercado[53] is in this neighbourhood and I'd go every day to do the shopping. I met a woman there who did the laundry and ironing in the house of some whites, she was from San Luis. She had a little daughter who she couldn't take with her to work, her bosses wouldn't let her. The little girl was called Silvia. I offered to take care of her and she was at my house for several years.

In the Plaza, I met all kinds of people and made friends with lots of prostitutes. I got to know different aspects of poverty and, especially, the different ways poor people found to make a living, by living, I mean subsistence. There was everything: stalls with cooked food, vegetables, fruit, butchers with every kind of meat, fish stalls, chicken stands, really, everything. You could buy anything there – from a sewing needle to horse panniers. You'd meet a beggar one minute and a singer of *décimas* the next. Prostitutes, pimps, gamblers, pickpockets… every kind of business went on there.

But poverty could be seen in all its magnitude. Men and women delving into the piles of rotten vegetables, to be able, with a few *quilos*, to take something to eat to their children. The meat the poor bought was what they called *carne de soguita*, nothing more than the hide they'd cut off the strips of beef that had a few little pieces of meat on it. They used it to make soup; it was very cheap.

But there was more to see in the Plaza. Stalls where they sold second hand clothes and old shoes – well, out of fashion. They also rented men's suits for those going into the *Vivac* – the temporary prison, in the corner of the Plaza – because you couldn't go in there without a suit. It never occurred to me to ask why they had that requirement.

I always noticed how they sold school shoes – the ones some poor people wore. They'd make a hole in the heel and put a thick cord through to tie the two feet together, then they'd hang them from a pole; it looked like a tree in mourning. They were in competition with the sandal sellers. It's incredible, shoes cost ninety-nine centavos, and sandals fifty; and cheap as they were, there were an infinite number of barefoot children and men and women with heels flapping.

There was a famous place facing the Plaza: it was a Chinese restaurant called 'El Pacífico'. It was always full and they worked twenty-four hours a day; those Chinese people really cooked well. Many poor people ate there, because they sold a complete meal, all the food together on one plate, for only twenty *quilos*. The police were permanently in the Plaza to prevent robberies and fights, to pursue the numbers runners and those who bet on *charadas*.[54]

But who pursued them? Because they were the worst thieves, the most likely to be gambling, the most shameless. They had to be paid for everything. Everyone had to pay them: the numbers runners, the pimps; that's what the police were, they took care of 'order' all right.

The prostitutes

I met many people in the Plaza del Mercado, some of them with huge spiritual poverty; these were the prostitutes! They 'worked' at night and slept all morning, so they didn't cook. Since, in my struggle to make ends meet, I had set up a *tren de cantinas*[55] many of them came to get me to prepare their meals for them. That's how I met Dalia and Delia. So kind-hearted they were! They became very fond of my family, so much so that one baptised you and the other your sister Carlota. Lots of those women weren't bad. I would say almost all of them were victims of the system prevalent in our country.

The majority were peasants or from other villages. The pimps went to these places and seduced them, they'd bring the deluded girls to Santiago and then get them involved in that. I'm not justifying prostitution, one can always make one's way decently, but in that system everything was difficult. There was something I always noticed. There were white, mulatta and black prostitutes. The most sought-after were the white ones, but the most mistreated and worst paid were the black ones: not even for that did men much like black women.

Prostitutes had their own hierarchy. Some were set up in houses and carried on their activities there. Others lived collectively in brothels where they were exploited by the owner of the house – the madam – who was not usually an active prostitute herself. There were those who lived in tiny, dilapidated rooms, and those who worked in the dance academies.[56] They earned according to their category and led, from the economic point of view, a more or less difficult life. But they were all wretched, marginalized and discriminated

71

against. It was hard to understand how they could live that way.

I took charge of Bubú, who was the son of a prostitute. When I first took him home he was covered in spots. He was a lovely little blond boy. When he was cured he was adorable. Later they brought me Felito, also white. I didn't charge for taking care of them, just as long as their mothers helped me with the cost of feeding their children. What inspired me to do that was my feeling of humanity and sad memories of my own childhood. I raised twenty-one children like that, over a period of fifteen years. If I point out that some of those children were white, it's to emphasize that the fundamental problem in Cuba was not just being black, but being poor.

Of those children, the ones who were with me the longest were Marta's – an assumed name, because she's still alive and I don't know if she'd appreciate me mentioning her real one. I met her one morning when I was going up the steps to the Plaza. She was sitting there crying. I couldn't help but notice. A white girl, so pretty, why was she crying like that? I went over and said:

– What's the matter, dear?

– Leave me alone! Nothing's the matter with me, it's nothing.

– If nothing's happened to you then why are you crying? Go on, you can trust me! Tell me why you're crying, what happened?

Then she sobbed and cried even harder. I asked her:

– Do you want to come home with me? You'd be better off there than here.

And she answered me with a shrug of her shoulders meaning it was all the same to her. I went up to do my errands and when I came back down she was still there and I said:

– Come on, we're going to my house.

And when we got there, she started crying again.

– Tell me, tell me, dear, trust me, tell me what's happened.

– So many things, Señora.

– Would you like to have a bath and freshen up?

I prepared a warm bath for her. I gave her one of my housecoats and a slip to put on. I made her a good hot milky coffee. She drank it, got into bed and told me:

– It's been so long since I've had anywhere to rest or anyone to console me!

I stroked her head like this until she fell asleep. Two hours later when she woke up, she said,

– I don't know how I can pay you for this.

And then she told me what had happened to her. A very, very sad story. Oh my goodness, poor girl! She lived in Bayamo. She was very poor; she was divorced with three children: two girls and a boy, two, three and five years old. One day she met a man who told her that if she wanted to work in Santiago he could help her. She accepted and came here and that man brought her to a brothel.

The same old story: when her family found out, they spurned her. They wouldn't let her see her children. Since she wanted to have them with her, I offered to take care of them. They were with me until they left my house to get married. Marta got married too; she met a foreigner who'd come to Cuba to live and he fell in love with her and got her out of that business. They loved me and called me grandma. Those kids have grandchildren now. They're all very fond of me.

Rubiera didn't like that at all. He protested and tried to forbid it, but without result. I told him to think of his own children: if one day they found themselves alone, wouldn't he want someone to shelter them? And so on, until I convinced him… Or he gave it up as impossible. Moreover, he didn't maintain them or struggle with them. On the other hand, he wasn't as distrustful as he used to be with things to do with the house. But he never understood why I did all that, why I didn't

73

charge those women a single *centavo*. He never understood that I was a mother too, and what a mother's grief was. No he never understood that!

Silvio, Saraza and Juan Pesca'o

It was very common to see the *patos*[57] going up and down Barracones street. You know, they didn't have to declare themselves, they were easily recognized by their way of talking, walking and gesticulating, in short, they felt like women and acted as if they were. I had dealings with three of them, because they almost always ate in the little diner I had in my house. They were very calm and well behaved. Two of them were very cultured. I remember them so well I can almost see them: Silvio, Saraza and Juan Pesca'o.

Saraza was a hair-dresser, he had wonderful hands for his trade. He made a lot of money; just think, he was the hairdresser for the majority of the prostitutes. In those days lots of women wore ringlets and he did lovely ones. He was tall, dark and handsome, very refined; this came in quite handy for him as a homosexual. Saraza didn't like men to pressure him and if someone started some trouble with him, he'd say:

– How is it, then? Like a man or what?

And if the man urged him on, they'd often come to blows. He didn't like to be blackmailed for being homosexual. He said since he didn't bother anybody, they should respect him.

Silvio was a tall, good-looking mulatto. He worked in a warehouse. He was very polite and spoke very carefully. I never knew where he lived but after dark and on the weekends he was always around Barracones.

Juan Pesca'o was a tall, thin *jaba'o*,[58] very boisterous. He hadn't had much schooling but knew how to act outside the ambience where he lived as a homosexual. I didn't know what he did for a living or where he lived. My relationships with

74

them, as I said, were owing to the fact that they ate almost everyday in my little restaurant. Also, your sister Pura used to make the dresses they wore during carnival.

It was quite common for men to dress up as women in the carnival *fiestas*. This was an eagerly awaited opportunity for homosexuals to dress as women. They prepared carefully for these days. They bought wigs, high-heeled shoes, evening bags, fans, earrings, necklaces and the costumes they made – many of them – were lovely. There were those who made various different ones, for the *fiestas* lasted several days. Pura sewed for Silvio, Saraza and Juan Pesca'o. The costumes she made were long and fashionable. Lace, taffeta, tulle, nylon; in actual fact, when they went out in those getups, if you didn't know them, you'd think they really were women. But they couldn't hide their condition, precisely because of the type of clothing they wore. No woman would go out during carnival dressed like that. What is certain is that these types of people were typical of the Santiago carnivals up until 1959.

And they were famous

There was a tenement there in Barracones called 'La Salvación'. It was a big two-storey house with a wide front door and a big interior patio. The rooms were one beside the other, in a U-shape, upstairs and down. People of all sorts and all colours lived there. Sometimes there'd be a fight among families or between neighbours. And, occasionally, a big party.

I knew all the residents of 'La Salvación'. I met Olga Guillot[59] there, the one who later became a famous singer with a gold record and everything. One of her sisters lived there, they called her Cucha. Olga often came to visit her. When she was discovered as a singer and became famous, Cucha went to Havana too and we never heard anything more about her.

A married couple lived in 'La Salvación' for quite a while: Celina and Reutilio,[60] they sang *puntos guajiros*.[61] He played guitar and she the *clave*.[62] They sang in bars, businesses, parks and places like that and then they'd pass a box around to collect the money people gave for their performance. They were very young. One time they went to Havana, I think to enter a contest, or to perform somewhere. The fact is, they didn't come back. In time they became famous. You already know that Reutilio died, Celina continued her artistic career, first alone and later with her son. She's famous, very famous. The queen of *campesino* music. I like listening to her sing. I'm pleased that she prevailed and reached the top.

There were quite a few *trovadores*[63] who lived in that tenement; among them, one they called Cucho, *el Pollero*.[64] He was a very good singer and song-writer. He would rehearse in the patio of the tenement. On one occasion, I went to take some clothes to Cucho – because he was poor, but he brought me his clothes to spruce up for the places where he would sing, sometimes I'd have to mend them – and there was a young man, very young, who sang beautifully and was rehearsing with them. They introduced me. He stayed there for a couple of weeks. I washed some clothes for him twice. Who could have told me then that this young man would be famous not only in Cuba but all over the whole world. It was your idol, Benny Moré.[65] Remember when he came to play at Bayamo, back in nineteen fifty something, and you went off with your friends because you wanted to dance with him? And you did. You danced with Benny Moré! But what a job I had keeping your father from beating you to death, that was a scandal for him.

I know there are people who, when they achieve fame, don't like their past being discussed, if it wasn't perfect. But since I'm doing a balance sheet of my own, I'm satisfied to let it be known I knew them, that I knew those who later became famous.

The three kings

Since you're my youngest daughter you didn't share the sufferings of your brothers and sisters on *Día de los Reyes* – they always say it didn't last long because soon afterwards I'd cheer them up somehow, with some 'silliness'. You sure got presents for *Reyes*! By that time I'd figured out how to solve those problems.

But talking of earlier times, I did suffer on that day. There was one time when your sister Moña asked for a big, blond rubber doll, who opened and closed her eyes. What I could afford was a little bald one, who had her little legs stuck together, a few coloured feathers for a skirt, with bulging eyes and some big rings: one of those dolls they called *Abisinias*. She got very sad, but when she looked up at me, she seemed to understand, and she said:

– Mama, this isn't the one I asked for but, you know what? I like her better!

Those words lacerated my heart, but I held back and didn't cry. I loved my daughter even more that day, because I realized she'd understood the *Reyes* were me.

The same thing happened with my son Nené. He wanted a big horse with a long mane, and what the *Reyes* brought him was a stick with wheels at the bottom and a wooden horse's head with a string to pull it with. One year, Monín wanted two pistols like Roy Rogers had, with white handles engraved with a horse's head. My poor little boy when he saw the little cap gun with its shots you could barely hear! And Carlotica, with high hopes for her sewing – she loved embroidery – couldn't be happy with that little hoop with a piece of material, two or three needles and a few little spools of coloured thread.

It was awful for me, but one day I had a tremendous experience. It was like a lesson. I woke up very distressed that day, despite my efforts I couldn't buy any toys for your brothers and sisters. I cried and cried as day broke. Halfway through the morning, your brother Chichí fell and broke his arm. I took him to the hospital where they took care of poor children; while I waited for them to put the cast on, I went into a room where there were eight or ten children. They were lying in cribs that were in a terrible state, with filthy, grey sheets. They were almost all crying. One said to me:

– Señora, do you know my mama? Tell her to come and get me.

That broke my heart, such sad little faces. I ran off to look for my son. When I got home, I knelt down in front of my *Virgencita* and begged her forgiveness for my dissatisfaction. The children in hospital were much worse off than mine. Although thinking about it, it wasn't dissatisfaction: I just didn't want my children to suffer what I had suffered.

José María, 'Cuto'

I had two full brothers. Julián, who never lived with my mother, because he was always with my grandmother, Mamacita, until he got married and set up his own home, there in Cueto. He lived there till he died. The other, José María, we called Cuto. He always lived with my mama and suffered a lot due to her complexes: he was black-black. Through struggle and sacrifice he became a teacher. But after graduation he didn't practice teaching until after he was old. Since he didn't want to work out in the bush, he came to live with me in Barracones. He got a job selling medicine for a pharmaceutical company called something like *Wytone* or *Witone*, I can't really remember.

There was a time when he had to travel a lot to Haiti and Santo Domingo for his job. He was going to get married to a Haitian woman, but he couldn't. She was murdered by mistake, they confused her with another woman. My poor brother! He was so traumatized by that experience he never got married. He was always a rover but my house was sort of his home base.

He was very fond of me and adored all of you. When he took you out walking he'd ask you to call him papá; and then he'd grant your every wish. Do you remember? You lot made the most of it and got him to buy you all kinds of delicious little things.

One of the things I remember admiringly about Cuto has to do with your sister Moña's *fiesta de quince.*[66] She wanted to celebrate it but I couldn't. Your father didn't care about such things, he didn't think them necessary, the girl's hopes didn't matter to him. Just around then, Cuto had arrived from Haiti; he had money, but I was ashamed to ask him. About a week before her birthday, Moña came home from school shouting at the top of her lungs:

– Mama, mama, look what I found! I found it on Santa Rica hill.

It was a roll of bills. I couldn't believe it, I questioned her and questioned her, she said the same thing every time. She swore to God she'd found it. I made her take me to the place where she'd supposedly found it. After all that and after waiting a few days to hear if anyone had lost a sum of money, I decided to use it. And what better than to celebrate Moña's fifteenth birthday; Pura made her a beautiful dress.

She invited all her friends in the neighbourhood and from school. What a *fiesta de quince* Moña had! You couldn't remember that, you were just little. Three or four days after the party, Cuto went to look for the money he had put away, and he was missing the exact amount that Moña had 'found'. We called her and she confessed everything. I felt so ashamed and impotent in front of my brother that I recognize now I wanted to take it all out on Moña. I grabbed her to strike her, he didn't let me, well, he said:

– No, Reyé, I'm the one you should hit. If I'd given you the money for the fiesta she wouldn't have had to do what she

did. Celebrating her birthday was an important dream for her.
– That's how my brother reacted.

Another time I planned an outing to Los Coquitos beach,
where the poor went to swim. I made a cornflour pudding,
bread with cod fritters, *pru*,[67] and we went to the beach! Cuto
was very romantic, he liked to write poetry. That day, sitting
on a rock, while the kids swam, he got inspired and started
writing something, it was a parody, to the tune of *María Bonita*
– Agustín Lara's[68] song. He left a few days later and in his first
letter he sent it to me. A few little bits of the song come to
mind:

Remember that afternoon, María Reyita,
María Reyita,
María del alma.
Remember on the beach
the little girls having fun,
playing so sweetly.
Moña, a piece of wood for a toy
while the waves rocked her.
And while I looked at you, I say with emotion,
I was so moved …
…Later we went to La Maya
You remember María Reyita, María del alma,
what a pleasant outing, welcome memories,
of our own childhood evoked;
I carry it within my soul
as a memento to send you in this letter.
And I tell you, deeply moved, I tell you with feeling,
that you are my sister
the most loved.

My poor brother! My poor, dear little brother! He's dead
now.

Two competitions

You're all very intelligent, if only we hadn't been so, so poor, you'd all have been professionals! In that anxiety to 'be someone' each had their vocation, which, in the long run, not all were able to develop. In Barracones, there was a man from Havana, a travelling salesman called Félix Escobar, who used to eat at our house. He had two children, Felito and Martica, who always went with him.

Seeing him in that situation, I told him to bring them to my house until he found a permanent place for them. In time, he met a rich woman – called Herminia. I'm not sure what kind of relationship he had with her but what I do know is that the little girl was sent to the 'María Auxiliadora' boarding school and the boy to 'Don Bosco'. In gratitude, she also paid for your brother Nené to go to the same school, but as a day pupil. It was a school for middle class people, a very good school.

When Nené was in sixth grade, the 'Dolores' school held a writing and composition contest. The three top entries could study there for free until the end of their *bachillerato*. The competition was, first of all, on a municipal level, and then, province-wide. Nené entered. Your brother was so excited! He said:

– Mama, this is my opportunity! I'm going to win.

And he got stuck into studying night and day. In the municipal heat he came second. When he got home he said to me:

– You see, I told you this was my opportunity.

In the provincial competition he again won second prize. He had his place at school guaranteed until he finished his *bachillerato*. The day of the awards ceremony – how exciting! – he was so nervous. But we'd forgotten he was black; that was not a school for blacks, much less for poor kids. They changed his name for that of another child and gave him a José Martí book. We know who the other was but, why say his name now? Nené suffered a great disappointment; many, many days went by before he'd even speak.

You wanted to be a pianist, remember? I know you haven't forgotten the wooden piano with painted-on keys that your brother Monín made you and where you sat for hours and hours playing pieces, many of them invented, that you'd hum so they'd have music. What an effort you made to get classes with that private teacher! Dora Villafañe she was called.

I didn't realize that without having a piano it was impossible for you to learn. Your cousin had one, but she wouldn't let you practice in her house; she was very selfish, wasn't she? The unlikeliness of us buying you one was one of your reasons for giving it up, that was sad for both of us, but I know you were happy while it lasted. I'm sure you haven't forgotten the day you first sat in front of a real piano, Oh, my dear!

Later you wanted to be a singer, you were going to be an artist. I taught you a *bolero*, to sing in the *Corte Supremo del Arte* contest,[69] called *Toda una vida*. Moña sang that one, *Vereda Tropical*, but they gonged her because her voice cracked. But you won first place. You had to go to Havana for the national contest. But who 'put the bell on the cat': as was to be expected your dad wouldn't let you go, and he said to me:

– At this rate, Daisy won't stop till she's a whore.

I know you wanted to be an artist. If it hadn't have been for your dad, perhaps you might have made it. The *Corte Supremo del Arte* contest and the writing and composition one for Nené could have changed the course of your lives, because you both won hands down. But sometimes destiny thwarts us.

My will was done

'Who are you?' I asked two men who came through the yard into my house to hide because they were being chased; they were two members of the Popular Socialist Party.[70] I had heard a lot of talk about that Party, and what I liked most was that they fought for, among other things, equality between blacks and whites and between men and women. They told me a lot about the Party in the time they were there, I got excited and, shortly after, applied for membership through a comrade whose last name was Maceo – I already knew him, he ate in my little diner, but I didn't know he was a member of the Party – and they accepted me. That was in the 40s.

On one occasion they needed a secure place to hold a meeting, they raised the issue with me and I told them my house was at the Party's disposal. It wouldn't attract attention because my daughter Pura was a seamstress and had many clients, and lots of people ate at my place. That day I met many *compañeros*, Juan Taquechell, Elías Lega, Calderío, Urrutia. That was in the days of César Vilar.[71] I remember them well. There held lots of meetings in my house.

I carried out various activities for the Party; I remember selling vouchers, and the newspaper *Hoy*,[72] and holding little gatherings to raise money. Once they had a contest to elect a young mayoress, which turned into a *fiesta*, also to raise money, because everything we brought was for sale. At the corner of Barracones and Princesa they set up an Academy of Tailoring and Dressmaking; it wasn't very expensive but this money too was for the coffers. Your sister Pura collaborated by giving classes to the little girls who enrolled. I also attended meetings and activities outside of the house.

I led a very active life within the Party. Rubiera didn't like it at all, but I paid no attention to him. Already for quite a while I'd been busy with all sorts of things he didn't like, but it was that I was waking up – you know? – waking up from the blindness caused by my naïveté.

I remember one occasion when I was standing in the doorway and a nice-looking, swarthy young man passed by in the street and a prostitute, who was also passing, dropped a suggestion, and he was so rude to her. I couldn't contain myself and I called the boy to account. He wasn't bothered and we started to chat. He was a Chilean sailor, his ship was in port.

A few days later he came to the house to visit me and by coincidence Urrutia and Maceo were there. We got talking and found out he was in the Party too, in his country. We were just delighted. He told us about his experiences and we told him ours. I remember him so well, his name was Rafael Salazar. That was wonderful, struggling for equality, brotherhood, the rights of women. It was like a huge hopefulness was reborn inside me! But, of course, the struggle was not an easy one, there was a lot of sleaze in Cuban politics and that Party didn't go along with it. I never dropped out, but when I moved away from the city I lost my connections, honey, I lost my connections.

Man does not live by bread alone… nor does woman!

Rubiera was very conscientious when it came to the house, but he had his own criteria of what was important and what was necessary. I had bread, milk and coal delivered; I had a *libreta* to buy on credit at the shop and the butchers; in this sense we didn't have problems. But 'man does not live by bread alone'. That wasn't life.

I accepted your dad as a man, I respected him, I led a calm life with him – too calm, for my liking. I always thought life couldn't just be washing, ironing, cooking, and all the household chores. And that's what I had, but it wasn't what I wanted. I was very young then, and so I liked other things: going out, being entertained. But without Rubiera's authorization I shouldn't go out, but that only lasted up to a point!

Before we moved to Barracones your dad would go from the house to work and from work home again; but when he started working at the *Expreso Velar*, his relationship with his bosses and the other white employees made him change a lot. When he'd get home from work, he'd wash, eat and sit in a rocking chair to smoke, and your brothers and sisters would take turns keeping him cool with a fan. I didn't like that. The only one who didn't was you, remember what you said to him?

– None of that, I may be black but I'm no slave.

He went all red and told me:

– Mima, I'm gonna knock this little *negrita*'s teeth out.

But he never struck you, oh, but if he'd tried it… I wouldn't have let him.

He got along very well with the owner of the company, he was always going to visit him. However, they never came to my house nor did your father ever take me to their house; that hurt. I never reproached him, I needed to preserve my marriage, whatever the cost. He even changed his way of dressing, he wore undershirts with gold buttons, very fine clothes and shiny leather slippers. On the other hand, we barely had clothes to cover us or shoes on our feet. That didn't frighten me, it's why I began my struggle. Rubiera guaranteed – above and beyond his representation as head of the family – house, food, doctor and medicine. The rest I decided to go after myself.

Time went by. I was awakening, I wanted my children, those who were old enough, to study or learn a good trade. So I began to make a life, up to a certain point, independent of your old man's. We got along well, I'm sure he loved us, but he didn't see beyond his nose. I intended to get you out of that neighbourhood, and I never stopped explaining to him that this was imperative, that it was important to have a better atmosphere for our children. By dint of so much insistence –

or because I wore him down – we moved to Cristina street between Gasómetro and Callejón de Cobo. That was in 1950.

It was a big, pretty house, with an entrance off one street and another at the back; it was built of masonry with a broad front window; it had an excellent lay-out: living room and parlour together, then a big yard with lovely climbing lilacs. The bedrooms were on the left and the kitchen and dining room in the back. He paid quite a high rent for those days, but it was a good house. It was in a neighbourhood of middle-class and poor people, but almost all white.

I arrived there having decided to give my life an overhaul and, therefore, yours as well. Barracones stayed behind with its prostitutes, its pimps, the yankee sailors, hustlers, delinquents, and everything all that meant.

Chapter 3

What rock, what word, what consolation
can anyone offer?
Who can fathom the depth of this sorrow
who has never kissed the stars?

The promise to Saint Lazarus

In 1952 Rubiera had a duodenal ulcer which burst, despite the treatment he'd received. When I saw him with that huge haemorrhage, I went crazy. And before taking him to the hospital, I knelt down and begged for his life and his health, but not to my *Virgencita*, but rather to Saint Lazarus,[73] a saint who frightens me with his sores and flies. I promised him if he saved my old man I'd put him in the front hall of my house facing the street sharing the position with the Virgin of Charity of El Cobre. An awesome pledge, if you take into consideration that he wasn't the saint of my devotion! That's why I had faith he would help me. Your dad was saved and I fulfilled my promise when I moved to Bayamo a little while after the old man's illness.

I set up a very large altar, almost reaching the ceiling; we made a fine cape for the saint and I always had lots of flowers and candles for him. You kids didn't like it – you hadn't been raised with these beliefs, but with the holy fear of God, you practised Catholicism, were baptized, took communion and were married in the church – but you respected my decision. Also for this reason I made sure it was pretty, as if it were a decoration. Then came his saint's day. The 16th of December, the eve of the celebrations, besides flowers and candles, we gave him fruits, candies, rum, tobacco, a platter with basil leaves and an empty glass into which I threw a few coins.

The ceremony held on the eve of the saint's day fiesta is called the wake; I held one for Saint Lazarus. At midnight on that day not one more soul would fit in my house. Your dad was furious, he didn't believe in anything, my promise didn't matter to him and since he couldn't get me to get all those people out of the house, he went to sleep at the transport company, but not before hurling a string of foolish remarks at me.

At exactly midnight I asked the *Virgencita* for strength and clarity to attend to all those people and do what needed to be done in the circumstances, to which I was neither accustomed nor, therefore, prepared. We began with the orations I thought we should say and then sang a few prayers I knew. Then I began to *despojar*[74] everybody, and I started to feel some radiations that ran all through my body, something like shivers. I told each person what came into my head and recommended some cure. I finished very late and completely exhausted but I went to bed satisfied at having fulfilled my obligation contracted to the saint when I'd made the promise.

In the morning your sister Moña, joking around with me, said:

– Hey, mama! If you keep fulfilling that promise you're going to get rich.

She said that because the money vessel had about a hundred pesos in it from what people had given to do their duty by the saint. That didn't matter to me, I couldn't charge for charity, but why deny it was very helpful. After that day news began to spread: 'What good vision that María has, the fat black woman with white hair'; I became the spiritualist of the day. Many people knocked on my door, I never said no to anybody. I still

Reyita in her nineties

Daisy and Reyita

Isabel, Reyita's mother

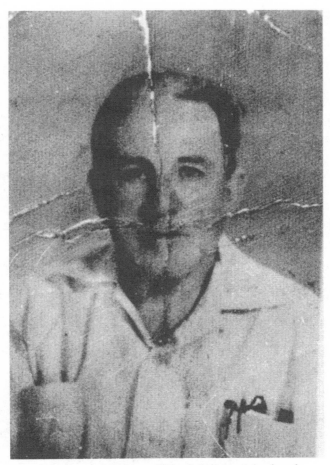

Antonio Amador Rubiera, 'Pancho', Reyita's husband

José, 'Pepe', older brother of Reyita, with his wife, Visitación Sánchez. He changed the family surname of his mother, as it was the slave master's name.

Isabel and José María, 'Cuto', Reyita's mother and brother

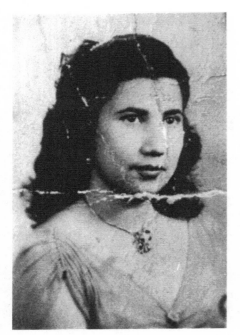

During the Barracones years, two of Reyita's friends, Delia (left) and Dalia (below)

Anselmo, 'Monín', Rubiera, Reyita's son

Moña in her satin dress

Antonia, 'Tata', third duaghter of Reyita

Reyita at fifty

Reyita at her daughter Daisy's wedding. On the right, Pura and her husband Ramón Moreno

Wedding of Pura (eldest daughter). From left to right, Rebeca, one of the children Reyita brought up; Maria Elena, her grand-daughter; three of her daughters, Carlota, Maria de los Angeles (Moña) and Daisy; Maria Antonia, Rebeca's sister

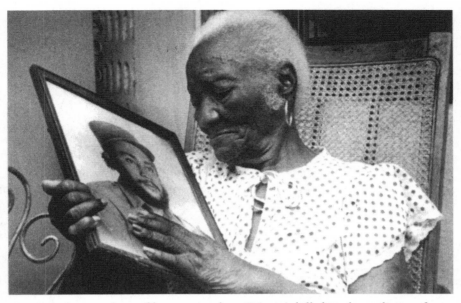

Reytia looks at a photo of her son Anselmo, 'Monin', killed in the explosion of battleship La Coubre in 1960

Reyita and sister Gloria

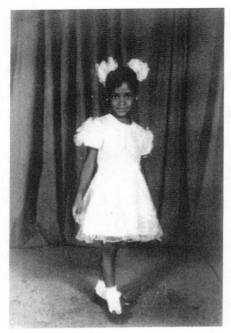

Dailys, one of Reyita's great-grandchildren

Isol and William Enrique, great grand-daughter and great grandson of Reyita

Reyima and Ana María, two more of Reyita's great-grandchildren

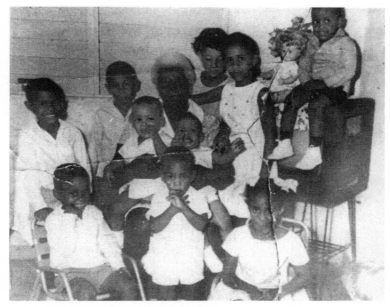

Reyita and some of her grandchildren

Carlitín, the grandchild who describes Reyita as the most beautiful grandma in the world

Anselmo, Monín's son, and Amanda, grandchild and great-grandchild

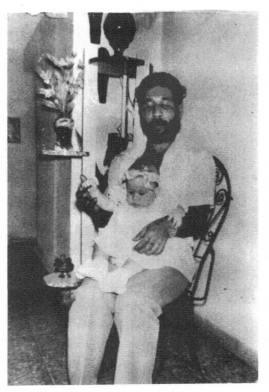

Reyita and baby Aníbal Antonio, number 118 of the family, and another grandchild, Reina Isabel

Above, Reyita and sons Chichí and Nené, below, with Nené

Above, Reyita with her sons and daughters, below, with members of the second and third generation

do it today although I'm old, with almost a hundred years behind me.

They call the spiritualism I practise *espiritismo cruza'o*.[75] People from Bayamo prefer *espiritismo de cordón;*[76] these believers, when they meet, join hands in a ring and sing and pray, while circling around the person they're going to consult or from whom they're going to remove a spirit. In this way they create a magnetic current which makes the faithful fall into trances. There were many of those places in Bayamo.

A long time before, I'd already had experiences as a healer with people other than my own family; I took my first steps when we lived in Cristina, here in Santiago, in about 1950 or 1951. Four or five houses away from mine, a doctor Portuondo had his consultancy; he was always telling me: 'María, don't get mixed up in all these cases, it'll only bring you trouble.'

Since my neighbours would come to my house for me to *sobar un empacho*[77] for their kids, bless them, cut an erysipelas – what they call lymphangitis these days – give them remedies for asthma, colds or diarrhoea, Portuondo told me that not actually to keep me from getting into trouble, but because I was taking clients away from him, who charged money or in kind. I, on the other hand, didn't want anything from anybody; I did it as an act of charity. Another thing Portuondo lost was the commission from the pharmacists, for the medicines he prescribed – shameless, they were! – sometimes they'd recommend more medicine than the patients needed, without taking into consideration their poverty.

Once a neighbour came to get me to look at her husband who had a bad stomach ache. I went with her, looked at the man, asked the Virgin to inspire me to alleviate his suffering and at that moment I had an idea: I told the woman to go get a bit of corn silk and I made an infusion. When she came back I gave it to the man. As soon as he took it he vomited up a ball that looked like the seed of a toledo mango – black with white

fuzz – and fainted. The woman, seeing her husband uncon-
scious, began to scream:

– You killed him, you killed him!

Not knowing what to do, I went to get Dr. Portuondo.

When he came and examined the man, he said he was alive,
and asked what I'd given him, and I explained. He put the ball
into a glass vial to send to a laboratory. I never found out the
result; the fact is, the man didn't die for another five or six
years, when we didn't live in that neighbourhood any more.

My visions

As a little girl I often had inexplicable visions. It was a
mediumship that I developed when I started doing spiritual
work, in Bayamo. I'd read a lot about spiritualism in the works
of Allan Kardec[78] and occasionally participated in this kind of
activity. That's how I could do what I did, although not without
certain insecurity and fear of making a mistake. I always thought
my *Virgencita* would help me to come out all right and
especially, be able to solve, to some extent, the problems of
those who came to my house seeking charity.

One day a man, who looked to be from the country, arrived
and said to me:

– Señora, I have a terrible problem. They told me you have
very good vision and I've come so you can help me resolve it.

– Come in and tell me what's the matter.

He was the foreman of a farm and he'd lost the blade of a
piece of machinery and he was almost sure a man who coveted
his position had taken it. His boss had given him three days to
find and replace it, or he'd be fired. What a problem for me!
But I thought any word of encouragement would stimulate
him to keep looking for the blade with more perseverance and
with more faith. I cleansed him, gave him some remedies to
do – I can't remember what – and he left, full of hope. On the

last of the three days the boss of the farm had allowed him, he found the blade hidden behind a big rock with tree branches around it. According to him, he'd already searched there several times.

He was so thrilled when he came to tell me about it, believing he'd found it due to the remedies I'd ordered. I think the belief that he'd find it was what made him scrutinize even the nooks he'd already searched. He brought me some chickens, vegetables and fruit as a gift; every once in a while he'd come to the house to bring me something, I always protested. The man from the clap-board house – as we called him – became a frequent visitor.

Another time a woman took me to look at her daughter, a little girl who was very sick; according to her, the doctor couldn't figure out what she had. I saw her belly was very swollen, I touched it and it felt very tense, she complained of pains and had a fever. The poor woman was desperate, someone had recommended me to her.

I remembered one of my granddaughters had had a similar condition not long before. I thought the girl must not have had very good medical attention – in those days, in the fifties, it was quite difficult for poor people. I cleansed both the child and her mother, and I gave her a little jar of pills for parasites; I think they were *tricomicida*, I don't remember exactly. I told her to give the little girl the same dose the doctor had recommended for my granddaughter. Since when people come looking for charity, they're not satisfied unless you recommend some remedy to do with religion, I prescribed some baths and prayers for the little girl.

A few days later the woman came to see me and told me the girl had passed a sac of parasites, her fever had broken and she was eating well. I was very pleased and recommended she take her back to the doctor. The little girl got to be so pretty. I think the experience of raising my own kids and all the other children I took care of helped me a lot in these types of cases.

Another time, a woman of about thirty – a *señorita*,[79] or so she said – came to see me. She had a boyfriend who hadn't decided to make their relationship proper, she asked me to perform a remedy that would tie the man to her. I looked at her and – I swear! – at the level of her belly I saw a 'little worm' moving around, and I said:

– Look, honey, you're not going to land that man, not with remedies and not with that child you're going to have!

– But María, what child? I'm a *señorita*.

– If you try to deceive me I can't help you.

She – so as appear to stand by her word, or out of shame, or for whatever reason – tore out of my house. About six or seven months later, Virtudes – that was her name – gave birth to a baby boy; the man left her when he found out she was pregnant because he was married.

The majority of people came to get the beneficence of the spirits, the dead or the saints when they were in difficulties, for health problems, justice, or to find a solution to a difficult or impossible problem they couldn't see a way out of on their own. In Cuba it's always been like this, and always will be: '*Aquí todo el mundo camina*'. [80]

My religious beliefs

The altar to Saint Lazarus made many things clear to me, but fundamentally, it helped me to define my religious beliefs which I could then develop in my own way, because I don't like going to ceremonies – not Santería ones or those of any other religion, including Catholicism. What I have done, once in a while, is conduct the *último rezo*[81] or last prayer for some member of the family or for friends, and provide charity to anyone who comes to my house seeking it.

When we moved away from Bayamo, my fame as a spiritualist stayed behind, but when I make a promise I stick to it, and so the altar to Saint Lazarus is still in my house, even after your dad's death. Did you know I still have a tiny altar in the corner of my room? And there it stays until the day I die. I still believe that charity should never be denied to anyone. Moreover, I always ask my Guardian Angel and my Protective Spirit to give me the clarity necessary to prevent any harm coming to any of you, because what I can be sure of is that while I'm alive anyone who tries will be wasting his time, and if they pay for it – because there are always unscrupulous people, who put their beliefs at the service of this rubbish – well, they'll also lose their money.

I've got lots of proof, I've seen and heard[82] a lot, things have become very clear to me. I've never been fanatical because I've read a lot about religion, and I've interpreted my readings from the point of view of my conviction that one must use all this knowledge as a guide, as a standard of conduct, and for me this is education: true faith lies in the confidence a man has in himself so that any help his Guardian Angel and Protective Spirit can give him will take effect. But of course, you've got to attend to them, they like and need to have a prayer or two every once in a while; you've got to light a candle so they can have light, give them flowers or simply a glass of water, and I say simply because it's the easiest to do, but water is very important to spirits, because it's their nourishment.

I have religiously followed the tradition of emptying a glass of water at the entrance to my house at midday, to nourish the spirits of my deceased loved ones. Because that's the time when they open the door of space, so they can go down and visit their families, and they need refreshment before coming in. When I started getting all the ailments of old age you used to do it for me, but since you moved to Havana and your sister Tata doesn't do it, I decided that my spirits had to move along with you, asking them to come and visit me after they'd had their nourishment. I'm sure they understood because when they get here I sense them and it's a bit later now, one or half past one in the afternoon.

I don't believe in miracles. I believe in the energy and clarity the spirits transmit to us, to enable us to take action in life and achieve what we want. Manna doesn't fall from the sky, honey, we have to look for it on earth, and look hard! I keep my religious beliefs to myself, as you know, because there are many frauds who take advantage of people to make money. I also think religion is an individual problem, each person should practise what they believe and what they want and how they want, as long as their beliefs don't do anyone any harm. Of one thing I'm sure and it's that in Cuba everyone carries his or her beliefs in their heart: whether they admit it or not.

And I had a gift

I began using home remedies, or herbal medicine, after I had you children. At that time health care in Cuba was very neglected: if you didn't have money to pay a doctor and buy medicines, then you could easily die, it was each to his own! Things were revealed to me in dreams, I had this grace or gift; that's how I received the knowledge to cure some pains. These cures always had some spiritual aspect: a bath with leaves or flowers or something.

You know I don't believe in miracles, but in the curative properties of the herbs and roots I used for those remedies, plus the faith and good will with which I made them: they were what really did the healing; I never worked with spirits, just with my inspirations; nor did I ever charge for what I did. I was born with this but I never considered myself a special person.

Now that I'm old I still attend whoever comes to my house looking for help. Mostly mothers who bring me their children so I'll rub out an *empacho*, or bless them because someone's put an 'evil eye' on them. Doctors don't recognize the *empacho*. This is nothing more than something they've eaten, that's given them indigestion and stuck in their stomach. It's easy to fix: you pass your hand – smeared with a bit of oil – from the pit of the stomach downwards, but gently; then you pull the skin of the back, over the spinal column. If the person is really *empachado*, you crack it three times, then they have to drink three mouthfuls of water, and the problem is solved.

The 'evil eye' – which is the depressive state one falls into when they've been *elogiado*[83] by one with evil vision – is removed by cleansing the victim, while reciting the oration to Saint Luis Beltrán. Animals and plants can also get the 'evil eye', in those cases the procedure is more complicated. It is a very bad thing, it can even kill.

I have a lot of faith in bee's honey: if you take a spoonful every morning on an empty stomach, you can avoid many illnesses. It can also prevent pregnancy; for this you dab some in the vagina and the spermatozoa stick to it and they can't get any further, so they die without reaching their destination. I told your sister-in-law Amalia this remedy after she'd had nine boys, because if not she was going to give birth to a whole army all by herself!

None of you had problems with puberty because I gave you blood tonics made with senna leaves and brown sugar. I put these in a jar, then topped it up with water and covered it with a piece of gauze, left it out in the sun and the night air for forty five days, and then I'd give you each a little glass before breakfast. You never had pimples or blackheads and none of you had problems with your periods.

There were a few asthmatics in our family and I cured them with a drink I gave them for breakfast, it's like coffee but made with toasted and ground palm nuts. Now I hear a lot of talk of scabies; we've never had that problem here because when it was going around the neighbourhood everyone in my family washed in water boiled with bitter broom leaves. Of course, you have to boil everything you use because it can come in off the street.

Nor did any of you suffer much from diarrhoea, because at the first sign I'd give you an infusion of guava sprouts, pomegranate and plantain stem; when my babies were a few months old I always gave them infusions of Castilian rose petals. I never had problems with lice; one of you got them once and I quickly prepared a bottle of alcohol with pig's bile – I left it for three or four days – and then scrubbed the scalp of each and every one of you, those that had them and those that didn't, I poisoned all your scalps so I wouldn't have to worry about that again.

When you became mothers you always trusted me to help you cure any little pains your children had, especially thrush – stomatitis – I got rid of it with one little treatment of mulberry leaf juice with a tiny pinch of bicarbonate of soda. Same with impetigo, you can get rid of this by cleaning with water boiled with white oleander leaves, which to my mind is better than *agua de Alibour*.[84] When you were little I liked to bathe you in water that had been boiled with sweet potato vines, that's why I didn't have to fight off pimples or rashes, that's why you've all got such lovely, smooth skin.

I've helped many women to get pregnant who couldn't have children – whether them or their husbands – with a remedy that both have to take. You make it in the following manner: you put four strips of charcoal wood into a jar, add seven spoonfuls of brown sugar and fill with water, tie a piece of gauze around the top to cover it and leave it be for forty-five days in the sun and the dew. After this time you start to use it and each takes a small glass on an empty stomach. You know it works because after ten years of struggling with your son Vivi, we gave them the remedy and along came Aníbal Antonio, my great-grandson! – the one hundred and eighteenth member of this family.

Now I'm going to tell you a story that's nothing more than an old woman's wickedness. Your niece, Reyita, had a friend who went with her boyfriend, but that relationship didn't end up lasting and about three or four months later she came home. A while later she fell in love again, this time with a boy who had good intentions toward her. Whether out of prejudice or fear of losing him she didn't tell him about this other relationship and the boy thought she was a *señorita*. As the wedding day approached, she didn't know what to do so she told Reyita, who was the only one to know of her worries. Your niece said to her:

– I've got a grandmother who knows lots of things, let's go see what she can do for you.

– No way, I'd be too embarrassed.

– No, *vieja*, you'll see, my grandma's my grandma.

She convinced her in the end and brought her to see me. She put me in a terrible fix but something occurred to me and this is what I recommended:

– The day of the wedding – I told her – you'll need to have a fresh chicken liver. Seven days before, start cleaning yourself with alum water, only seven days, no more, because any more and poor you! The day of the wedding, when you go on your honeymoon, take the chicken liver, well hidden. When you go to wash before getting into bed, put it up in your vagina. The rest, you already know!… don't think about it, just enjoy the moment. When you come back, come and see me and tell me how you got on.

– *Vieja*, you think it'll work?

– Yes, child, do it with faith and you'll see, everything'll be fine.

When she came back, the girl arrived at my house covering me with kisses from the moment she saw me, because everything went just as planned. That had nothing to do with the gift I was born with; that was the result of experience, of the years, of having seen and heard many things... besides, it was a bit of a dirty trick. The girl went along trustingly, so her nerves didn't give her away. She abandoned herself to the pleasure happily and in the heat of the moment the boy didn't notice she wasn't a virgin. I still heal and give advice. Thank God everything I recommend turns out all right. You know what they say: 'more of the devil's knowledge comes from his age than his job.' In my case, I know more from being ancient than old, and because I'm still 'alive and kicking'.

Love comes in through the kitchen door

Although it's not for me to say, I was an excellent cook. Not fancy cuisine with creams and roasts, but I was quite an expert in traditional Cuban food. In the first place I love doing it; in the second, I had a very fussy husband in that department; in the third, because for a time I made my living with little diners and take-aways. But moreover, eating is bliss, ah, eating is a wonderful pleasure!

I invented a *malanga* pudding (see note 20), which you and your dad all liked very much. Remember how to make it? No? What a scandal! Women aren't too keen on cooking these days – and just when they don't have so much choice – well, I'll remind you.

You boil the *malangas* with a little salt, and then purée them, add milk boiled with cinnamon, anise, nutmeg, cloves, vanilla, white sugar, to taste, and butter. After you've got it all blended, you pour it into a pan greased with butter. You put it on the fire over a slow flame and cover it with a lid filled with hot coals so it gets golden brown on the top and the bottom; if you've got an oven you can bake it. Take it off the heat after thirty or forty minutes. Let it cool and turn it out onto a serving plate. It's delicious!

All of us are soup people, we really like it. There are so many soups: from the exquisite chicken soup to the traditional Santiago *ajiaco*. These ones go without saying, but one I have to remind you of is the delectable garlic soup. It's so easy to make. You need: slices of bread, garlic, sweet peppers, bay leaves and eggs. Toast the bread, crush the garlic well and put it to boil with the bay leaves and the sweet peppers; add salt to taste. When that's boiled for quite a while, add the toasted bread and leave it on the heat for a couple of minutes. Take it off. And when serving, add a raw egg to each bowl, stir well, and it's done! It's a delicious soup, nutritious and very soothing to the stomach.

Here in Santiago, poor people would often make stone soup. When things were really bad and there was nothing to cook, you'd put a pot of water on the fire and – since we lived in a real collective – you'd say to your neighbours:

– I'm going to make a stone soup.

Or they'd ask you:

– Reyita, what are you going to cook today?

– I don't know, honey, I think I'll make a stone soup.

And whatever the case, pretty soon the solidarity would swing into action.

– Well, I've got some *malangas*, I'll give you…

– I've got potatoes…

– And I've got some joints of salt pork…

And so on and so on, you'd get all the things you needed to make, not a simple soup but a terrific *ajiaco*. I gave lots of ingredients for my neighbours' stone soups – mostly when we lived in Chicharrones – but I'm not embarrassed to say I also had to make my share of them.

Santeros[85] say the saints, or *orishas*, eat. I don't know anything about this. But I've got my Saint Lazarus and if they eat, I can't let him starve out of my ignorance. But since I don't want to take a course in ritual food either, I give him sweet corn on a plate, sometimes I toast it, and on festival days I give him candies and fruit, as well as his cigar and glass of rum because he loves that! I do it willingly and I think he understands.

I do the same with my *Virgencita*, so she doesn't get jealous; she gets honey and squash. Why these things? Because I read it in a book that explained the different foods to offer the saints. Since I do it with faith and love, I know they receive it gratefully, and enjoy it with satisfaction.

In search of a better life

In the fifties there was no lack of anything in Cuba, the shops were full of all the things anyone could need. What was missing was the money to buy them. The jobs available paid very low salaries, that couldn't make ends meet. Those without much education, and this was the vast majority, were paid miserably if they managed to get a job. There were many people who worked for themselves, mostly selling things like vegetables, fruit, home-made candies, newspapers, lottery tickets, and shining shoes, and innumerable other things; and in their houses, the stove was cold until they got home.

It was quite common back then for the neighbourhood shops to close a little late and for their owners to live in a room off the back the shop. The majority of their customers were street pedlars who bought food on their way home, with the money they'd made during the day; then they'd knock at the shopkeeper's door, who'd willingly open up to serve them. They didn't always do so out of understanding, but because they depended on these men. Some sold on credit, and so many neighbourhood shopkeepers went bankrupt, they were human and very trusting, despite those famous signs they put up saying: 'No credit today, try tomorrow'.

In 1953 they offered your dad a job as Agent of the *Expreso Velar* and *Expreso Alvarez* transport companies in the city of Bayamo. He accepted, it came with a better salary and he could employ your brothers Monín and Nené there. What I didn't like about it was that Nené had to give up studying for his *bachillerato*. Rubiera said bachelor or not, it was all the same, the best thing for the boy was to have a steady job. They went ahead, to prepare for the move, and the old man sent money each month for expenses: rent, electricity, groceries and any medicines we needed.

At that time I was deeply in debt, it was not long after your sister Moña's wedding. But since I wanted to buy some new things for when we moved – it was three months before we went – I bought them with the money he sent me. But, what sacrifice! We'd have one meal a day, corn flour with mince meat, at night milky coffee and bread with whatever there was, almost always cod fritters; you used to call this meal 'nocturnal breakfast'. You, Carlota, and the three children I was taking care of that I already mentioned, were at home then.

You bunch were terrible! When your dad sent word he was coming to get us, you made up a very funny verse that went:

Good job Pancho's coming now
if not he would find
his children had turned yellow
from all the flour on which they'd dined
Mami, don't get all dressed up
in colours so combined
you've spent Daddy's money
on fabrics so divine
and if my Daddy finds out
he'll take it out of your behind.

Finally Rubiera arrived. I'd saved a few *quilitos* to make a good meal and promised a spanking to whoever dared to recite the verse to him. A week to pack up everything and back I went to Bayamo, so many years after I'd left. We were in search of a better life.

The house we moved to was in a street called Tienda Larga (Long Shop) – remember how we laughed at its silly name? That house was small and uncomfortable. By protesting to your dad, we managed to move to a bigger one a few months later. It was on Zeneda street, quite close to the transport company where the old man worked.

I was three or four days without sticking my head outside the door, getting my house in order, and singing while I bustled about. The first day I went out to the sidewalk to sweep it the woman next door – Leo, remember her? – asked me:

– Is Rubiera's wife in?

– That's me.

– ¡*Caramba*! I heard you singing and you've got such a lovely voice, I thought you were white.

What a way to think! So, you couldn't have a nice voice if you were black? – with all the great black Cuban singers!

Bayamo reminded me of when I'd lived there before, but now the situation was different: Rubiera was Señor Rubiera, the Agent of an important transport company. He had his world there but without neglecting his family. Other things still didn't matter to him.

I always tried to keep the shade of discrimination from falling on you, my children, so it bothered me when some businessmen – who your dad dealt with – called someone by saying: 'Hey, blackie', 'Come here, *negrito*', not in an affectionate tone but somewhat scornfully.

Nobody would dare say anything of the sort to any of you in front of me, because I, in the nicest possible way, and always with a smile on my face, would put anyone in his place. You had to be respected and, naturally, you had to respect others. And thus, during the time we lived in that city we managed to make friends with everyone.

As far as relations with the businessmen and everything to do with the company went, you know I directed the boys to go there just to work, because money and colour create enormous differences: therefore a white man with money was no friend of a poor black man. There were exceptions, but the rest was just politicians' hot air to assure themselves of votes, and fairy tales.

I had never fought with your dad; my problems with him started in Bayamo, because he wouldn't let you or your sister even breathe. If I let you go to the pictures or some little party, he'd say:

– Mima, you're going to let those daughters of yours become sluts.

We argued about this, time had passed, life changed, I didn't want you and Carlota to have to live the convent life like the rest. He put brakes on your social lives.

Time went by, the political situation of the country was very difficult. Batista's dictatorship was horrible. Every morning would bring young corpses, just dumped anywhere; the *guardia*[86] did what they liked, mistreated people and beat them up for any little thing. There was terrible poverty; the unsanitary conditions in the poor neighbourhoods were alarming; many children didn't go to school; there was no work and no social security whatsoever. That's how things were in Cuba in 1958.

Down with the dictatorship!

One day, I accidentally overheard a conversation between your brothers Monín and Nené and realized they belonged to the 26th of July movement.[87] I didn't want to be indiscreet but I started to help them, without their knowledge; I'd explain away their night-time absences from the transport company to their father, so they could do their part for the revolution.

I had to live with a double anxiety then: the struggle for subsistence – which at that point wasn't so bad, because your father was making good money – and that of knowing the danger your brothers were risking. But always with the certainty that my *Virgencita* of Charity of El Cobre would not abandon them, would protect them for me, and all tinged with the grand hope that the triumph of the revolution would bring a better life.

One time the boys were arrested. What an awful torment, my God! Those *guardia* were beasts, taking a revolutionary prisoner, torturing and killing him were all the same to them. We had to move fast. We managed to get them out of prison by negotiating with the city's Mayor, through one of his sons who was at school with you. Do you remember that horrible time? Monín was tortured. A few days later, Monín received orders to join the fighters in the hills; he made use of a truck that was in the transport company full of goods and took it into the Sierra.[88]

From that moment on the situation became very tense for us. Rubiera was always very cowardly; he found out his sons were in the 26th of July Movement when Monín went to the mountains. He wanted to die – and to kill me. He said it was my fault for putting strange ideas into the boys' heads. Captain Morejón, chief of the Bayamo garrison, didn't take his eyes off us, especially your brother Nené who, thanks to a warning they were going to kill him (sent by a *guardia* called Peruchín), left Bayamo that very night in the middle of a downpour; he went to Captain Bárzaga's camp, where your other brother was.

The case of Peruchín was very common. Poor boys without work, practically illiterate, obliged to sign up for the army in order to survive, where they earned a pittance, but it was a steady salary. Many acted properly, fulfilling their duty. Others turned bad, became dehumanized, even beat up their child-hood friends. They abused the shopkeepers, taking things with-out paying for them, took money from the numbers runners, instead of arresting them; blackmailed the pimps and prosti-tutes; in short, a complete degradation which, in many cases, went as far as cold-blooded murder.

After Nené went up, they searched our house and since they didn't find anything compromising, started spying on us. It was the baker who did it. They used to call him '*pan pan*', because that's how he announced his wares. In time he was found out to be a stool-pigeon who passed himself off as a revolutionary. But one day he went up to the Sierra with a message after he'd been found out and was tried and executed.

I calmed down a little when your sister Tata and Teresita – Nené's wife – went to the Sierra to see the boys. They weren't scared, they got round the soldiers by going through the bush, on foot, till they arrived at the camp where they were. They were there for several days. They came back happy, though protesting they hadn't wanted to come back but to stay there. But the boys made them come back, because they thought I wouldn't be able to stand so much strain and worry. It was a great joy to me to know they were okay.

Your dad's situation got very difficult. As far as I understood, the company he worked for was owned by one of Batista's sons. He was very worried about our life, because since they couldn't get the boys the *guardia* wouldn't leave us alone; and since we lived close to the headquarters, we couldn't help but see them every day. Rubiera decided to change jobs and move back to Santiago. And so he did. One day he loaded all of us and a few of our things into one of the company's trucks, closed up the house and away we went. That was the day before they closed off the Central Highway to thwart the rebel advance on Santiago. We arrived there practically empty-handed with a little money your dad had, to get us set up. Thus was the sentence 'happiness is short-lived for the poor' carried out, and that was how long the better life we'd gone looking for in Bayamo lasted.

Chicharrones

Your dad rented a house in Chicharrones, a very poor neighbourhood they used to call the 'little Sierra' because of the number of members of the 26th of July Movement there; also because, in the middle of all that poverty and misery, the residents had all their hopes pinned on the revolution and because the bestiality of the regime put the lives of almost all the inhabitants in danger, revolutionaries or not. You could get to a nearby mountain range from there pretty easily so the neighbourhood was on the regular route for revolutionaries going to one part of the Sierra. The *guardia* and the police didn't like to enter this neighbourhood at night, they were scared.

Chicharrones was a very special neighbourhood: its streets – almost all of them – were steep, unpaved hills, from which you could see almost the whole city and part of Santiago Bay. There was no drainage system or running water, they brought it in big tanks and there would be huge lines of people waiting to fill the barrels, one pail at a time. Many houses were wooden with zinc or tar paper roofs; there were also some masonry ones with tiled roofs. But most were little houses made of pieces of wood and tar paper with dirt floors. There were also lots of tenements.

Everyone was poor in that neighbourhood and almost all were black. Your dad got a not very well-paid job at a little transport company called Meteoro; our economic situation was very difficult, he had nothing to do with anybody, living in a world I sometimes considered unreal. He'd come home from work, eat, sleep, sleep and eat and not meddle in any of the problems of the family.

You were the only one studying then. My God! What a worry: when it cost three *pesos* to register for the Institute and we couldn't pay it and had to apply for them to waive the fees through the Student's Association, how on earth were we going to afford university tuition, which was much higher? In order to survive I started a little fee-paying school and we took in sewing and made little plaster squares to sell...

My mama died around that time. I really felt the loss but I also felt fortunate, despite the sadness, to have been able to be with her during her final illness, at her side, until she closed her eyes. Since then the links with my maternal family have dwindled down to seeing each other now and then. We don't love each other any less even though we rarely see each other. Now there's only your aunt Gloria and I left.

That stage of my life wasn't very different from earlier ones. Rubiera and I got along almost like brother and sister, but I had so many other things going on in my life, worrying about that became a secondary concern; he never stopped making love to me, though not as regularly as he used to.

Chicharrones, like any poor neighbourhood, made us all live as one big family: we helped each other out with all our needs, which were many. I had two neighbours with lots of children and no husbands, who worked at whatever they could; neither of them could read or write.

Two doors down from my house was a little green grocer's and their children argued over the scraps of fruit and other things the clerk would throw away. One of these kids was called Cocó. One day, when I went into the grocer's to buy something, I saw him eating out of the bin and since then, whatever was cooked in my house, however little there was, I always put some by for Cocó. Despite all the years that have gone by, he's still in touch with my family.

I know you remember how things were in those days. And I thank God that you, even at the worst of times, always had something to eat, even if it were only flour and mince. And even though a yard of material cost twenty *quilos* – back then we measured in yards not metres – and they were poor quality materials, (because silks and lace weren't within reach of the poor) none of you ever went naked in that time when the majority of the population were badly clothed or in rags.

In Chicharrones they played a lot of *bolita* and *charada.*[89] Poor people, with the hope of winning a little money, ended up losing the little we had, and I say we because I played too. I was lucky and won many times, but never very much because I couldn't bring myself to put more than a *medio* on one number: three *centavos* fixed and two running. The money we lost went to line the pockets of the crooks who ran those businesses.

When the revolution triumphed I was living in that same neighbourhood. I taught a few people to read during the Literacy Campaign.[90] I had to do it in the neighbourhood, I couldn't go out to the country. I loved doing it; of course, since I enjoy learning so much, how could I not want to teach others! Know who my first students were? – my neighbours, the ones I mentioned before. The October Crisis[91] also found me in that neighbourhood. I worked very hard alongside the *compañeros* in the Revolutionary Defence Committees[92] collecting wood, axes and machetes. I also took a course in first aid: we had to be prepared for whatever might happen. Those were very tense moments, but we were firm and determined to defend our independence and our sovereignty.

Fears and fancies

I've never been a fearful person; as a little girl I used to like to sit out in the yard and look at the stars, I'd imagine they were greeting me, like when a person winks at you. But I am scared of thunder, lightning and snakes, especially *majá*.[93] If there's anything I find repulsive, it's frogs and cockroaches. I had a fight with one of my neighbours in Banes because, knowing I hated frogs, one day he brought me a paper cone, closed up tight, and said:

– Look, Reyita, I've brought you some nougat.

– Thanks, Edilberto.

Ay, muchacha! I opened it and stuck my hand in – without looking – I felt something cold and when I pulled it out, it was a frog. Ugh! I'll never forgive him.

You have to be careful with mice. Out there in the countryside, they slip into your bed and gnaw at your toes, and since they blow while they eat, you don't feel it.

I'm more than afraid of *jubos*.[94] Those animals are freaks; thank goodness they only live in the wilderness and life has modernized a lot. It's not so dangerous any more.

Imagine! They say shortly after women had given birth, *jubos* would come up into the bed. The *jubo* put the woman out[95] with its breath, and she'd go into a deep sleep; then it would put its tail in the baby's mouth so he thinks it's a nipple and doesn't cry. And meanwhile, they drink the mother's milk. Deep in the countryside, there were many such cases when I was a child.

The people I like least in the world are thieves and kleptomaniacs. The first are shameless and the second sick. There was a song, remember? It went ...*she was a kleptomaniac/ ...she stole for a thrill /...an urge she just couldn't still...*[96] Something like that, I can't remember. I like honest, trustworthy people, who get along with everybody, uncomplicated people.

I also like telling and to be told stories. All kinds! Heh heh. I'm going to tell you a real old one.

Once there was a married couple from Haiti who lived way out in the bush. When they came to town one time they met another couple and invited them to come to their house.

The next Sunday they went along and the Haitians went out of their way to make them welcome, especially with the meal. The invited couple decided to return.

The next Sunday the Haitian woman hears a song, which she didn't understand but, what a surprise! It's their friends who've come to visit again. Once again they eat wonderfully well.

And so on and so on, Sunday after Sunday; and they always arrive singing.

One day the woman pays close attention to the song and says to her husband:

– Ey, Manué, 'ave you 'eard what deez people come singin'?

– No, woman, what dey say?

– '*Vamo a case lo bobe*, we're goin ta stupids house,' Can't you 'ear?

– Ah, yeah woman, dat's it ezackly.

– You go to da kitchin, get dat pot off da stove.

And when the visitors arrive with a big smile, the Haitian woman begins to sing:

– Stupids now are knowin, stupids now are knowin.

They don't even offer them coffee, don't humour them at all and they get them off their backs.[97]

I liked being taken to wakes out in the country. It was a happening; the whole neighbourhood would get together, especially at night. The most distant relatives of the deceased were the ones in charge of making the *ajiaco*, and what a fabulous soup it would be! – it'd revive the dead if they'd given him any. That was to get through the night, lots of coffee, tobacco and once in a while you'd see a bottle of rum being passed around.

Then after midnight everyone would get into little groups and tell stories to keep each other awake. And what tales they'd tell, every kind of story you could want! They played lots of nasty practical jokes, putting lit cigars in the mouths of people who had fallen asleep, lit matches in their shoes. The limit was one time when they tied a hemp rope around the waist of the corpse, nice and tight. They did that during the day and then, late at night – wham! – the dead man sat up in his coffin. Feet, what are you doing there? – everyone ran for dear life; even his relatives ran, they left the dead man sitting up there alone like a general in his coffin.

No, I didn't see it, I heard the grown-ups talking about it in my house. Hey, I'll tell you something, when four or five old folks would get together to chat, they'd say the wildest things!: opinions, ghost stories, myths, I think even some fibs. There's lots of other things I like, reading is one of them. Now I'm rereading the Bible. I like listening to the radio, I love the soap operas on radio and television; the Brazilian ones they have now are really entertaining. I like the advice programmes; when I listen to them I feel better, they make me feel like new.

When the earth trembles

I'm not afraid of tremors. There was a very big one when I was little, but I don't remember it; in this part of the country, there are a lot of tremors. People think they're used to them, but it's not true, when the earth trembles no one stays calm: people always run out into the street, and it's the most dangerous place to be, because of electricity cables and the big trees on the sidewalks. Others fall to their knees to beg for mercy, it's chaos... when the earth trembles!

Here in Santiago there've been several big tremors, I'd say they were earthquakes! I remember a really big one in the thirties and another very strong one in the forties; that one wasn't just one jolt, but several, it trembled more or less strongly every so often for three or four days in a row. When I was younger I used to like to sit on the ground to feel the effect, so it would pass through me and I'd be left with that feeling... I don't know, but it never provoked in me the terror it seems to cause other people; just the opposite, I also like to put my feet on the ground to feel it. I lost my fear of them when we had the tremor of '32, yes, I think it was '31 or '32. And I haven't been afraid of them since.

Oh my God! – but do I remember that night: some screamed, some cried, others ran. That was the one in the forties, when we lived in Barracones. It was at night, we were just sitting talking in the front room; then, a tremor – have mercy! – and it passed, but about five minutes later came another one – *muchacha!* –there isn't a soul who wouldn't have started pleading for mercy. That was a very big tremor; your dad went crazy, he wanted to go out into the street, he wanted us all to go out but I said to him:

– No, not out the front door, no, because the electricity cables are out there and one of those wires could fall.

But he kept on, so I grabbed him like this, by the shoulders, I shook him, and I gave him a shove! I said:

– Out back, in the yard.

And we knocked down the sheets of zinc, the patio fence, and we all went out to the backyard. The house was on a very big lot, which actually belonged to three houses, it wasn't divided at the bottom – that was where they built the pharmacy *Mestre y Espinosa* many years later. Almost all the neighbours on the block took refuge in that lot. We made tents out of canvas – what they used to cover the loads on the transport company's trucks. Once we were out of the house I felt safe when there were tremors because all I was worried about was if the roof should fall in. Now that I'm old, I can't sit on the floor and what I do is just stay still wherever it catches me. I don't know why the earth doesn't tremble as much as it used to anymore.

Water and wind

Although earth tremors don't frighten me, cyclones send me into a panic. There aren't very many in this part of the country but the day Flora[98] went through, ¡mi madre! And when it went out and turned back in on itself, I don't even want to remember that! That was in 1963, I think in September or October, I don't remember exactly which month. Everyone was keeping their eyes on the weather forecasts on the television, radio and in the papers.

Once we were aware of the danger heading for us, we began to take precautionary measures: storing drinking water, getting to hand paraffin lamps, kerosene, matches, candles, hammers, nails and pieces of wood in case some door needed to be secured. We bought – within the possibilities of what could be acquired – biscuits, bread, vegetables, eggs; in short, we prepared for what was coming, for what we weren't used to, for the unknown, though it's not as bad as a tremor because at least you can take preventative measures.

The sky began to turn black, the rains came and the wind started up, everyone was so worried. We barely slept, it was like being on almost constant guard. I felt quite safe: my house was solid – bricks and cement – and in a place where flooding was out of the question. My children's houses weren't in danger either. But I suffered such terrible anxiety, what was going to happen? The newscasts were alarming. The government took all the necessary precautions to avert large-scale disasters. The

129

wind began to blow so fiercely it sounded like the roar of a lion, the trees beside the sidewalk in front of my house looked like they were about to come down. The torrential rains started; I don't know what did more damage, the water or the wind. That wretched cyclone didn't know when to stop.

I was so busy. All your sisters and brothers were mobilized by the militia,[99] you were the closest one I had; remember the afternoon we went under water to buy milk? That was terrible, the ditch flooded – that ditch is the city's drain to Aguadores beach. A man slipped and fell, and there was nothing we could do for him, the waters took him, the man drowned! That afternoon they began the evacuation of all the residents of Rebalisa.[100] They set up an improvised shelter in '30th of November' primary school. Luckily you were working there with other militia members, you were close to home and could give me and the kids lifts.

As well as looking after my grandchildren, I had to take care of a little girl who was in the school, because with all the humidity she caught bronchitis and only the most serious cases were being admitted to the children's hospital, there were so many. The country was a wreck, there were losses of every kind. But in spite of all those calamities we didn't lose faith or confidence... because after the water and wind pass, the sun always comes back out.

Iyá, la panza; panza, Iyá[101]

I love dancing, even though I've hardly ever danced, because my mama wouldn't let me and then, after I got married, even less, your dad didn't like parties. One time, back in La Maya, Isabel practically killed me. Across from the house where we were living there was a group of teenagers who'd get together in the evenings to play guitars, claves and drums. All the neighbourhood girls would come around to sing and dance there. I was just a little girl then, but I was drawn to them, I liked it. One day, while Isabel was at work, I snuck into the *cumbanchita*.[102] *Ay, muchacha!* I lost track of the time and just when I was having the most fun dancing around, I felt someone grab me by the ponytail and pull me; it was my mama! She shoved me away saying:

– You, as usual, playing the fool.

But some of my sisters were there too, and they didn't get dragged away.

I also liked the *comparsas*.[103] There were always lots of them for the San José *fiestas* in La Maya. One time my cousin Guarina and I joined one – when I was living with my uncle Juan. We were dancing along with one singing: *Iyá, la panza; panza, Iyá*. I was going along all crazed by the rhythm of the music. Then in one street I heard:

– What do you two think you're doing in that *comparsa*? Come away from there right now!

– And that was it, the *comparsa* was over for us. That ended up with an awful punishment.

I like carnival, it's a very cheerful *fiesta* and an especially collective one. Here in Santiago it was a very big event, people came from all over the country. There was a time when it went on for a month, then they started shortening it. Now it's only ten days or a week, but there's not the same splendour and colour as there used to be. I liked watching – from the door of my house – as the *mamarrachos*[104] went by.

The traditional neighbourhoods like El Tivolí, Los Hoyos, San Agustín and Trocha, all had their *comparsas*. They'd spend about a month rehearsing; they'd go out visiting other neighbourhoods, they called that the invasion – it was the clash of more than one *comparsa* – the ones from Los Hoyos and Paso Franco were the most traditional and historically rivals. When the *fiestas* started they paraded in front of the jury, with standards, banners, lanterns and, best of all, the wonderful,

131

infectious music with satirical lyrics, criticizing the situation up for discussion. All the *comparsas* kept a closely guarded secret: it would be a theatrical dance set, all of them aiming for first place. It was so exciting when they were revealed.

The *comparsas* spent the whole year saving money to buy their outfits: they would send out little cards – they sold them with verses printed on them – to a certain number of people, who would then become their godmothers or godfathers. They'd come to their houses on the day of the parade, and these would sew bits of coloured ribbons onto their costumes with money; they looked very pretty and eye-catching, some of the shirts were a mosaic of different colours, those were the ones with lots of godmothers and fathers who, despite being invisible actors in the carnivals, were the ones who put the finishing touches to the outfit of a *comparsero*.

The capes were an attractive aspect of the carnival parades; generally they were big and long, with some design stitched in with sequins, glass beads or shiny threads and with fringed edges; it was an honour for whoever wore it. There were beautiful, luxurious ones. The *capero*[105] was a very important person within the *comparsa* for the splendour of their capes. My cousin Chino was the *capero* of the Los Hoyos *comparsa*. Once he made one with the image of the Virgin of Charity of El Cobre on the back, lovely it was. Lots of people in Santiago wished they could have a cape for carnival, but they were very expensive.

The traditional streets of La Trocha and Paseo de Martí would be lined with kiosks – on the sidewalks, which are very wide – they were beautiful. These two neighbourhoods competed in this too, but la Trocha almost always won. They sold everything: beer, rum, bottled soft drinks, pork fricassée, *chilindrón de chivo*,[106] tamales, boiled root vegetables, *tostones*;[107] there were also little stalls selling cod fritters, patties, *mariquitas,*[108] fruit, *pru,* fruit drinks. Well, there was something for every taste and every pocket.

The streets of the different neighbourhoods were decorated with coloured paper, little lanterns, palm leaves, and lots of lights. Those ornaments hung from wires that crisscrossed the street and formed different shapes. The better and prettier they were, the better their chances of winning first prize; because they also judged the streets. There were some whose residents, as well as being enthusiastic, were very fastidious.

The shop windows would be decorated with carnival motifs. Carts passed through the streets selling whistles, noisemakers, masks, all kinds of hats, coloured batons, and cardboard or palm fans. Another very pretty sight was the carriages. I remember in the first carnival they held in Bayamo – because the traditional festival day there was Epiphany – that would have been '54 or '55, they went through the whole town with the ¡*Mulatas de Fuego!*[109] *Ay muchacha!* They almost caused the divorce of every couple there, because all the men were drooling along behind the carriage with those half-naked women. They were gorgeous!

Carnival was a bit of a hard time for me. Since Rubiera didn't like *fiestas,* he wouldn't let me go out; and much less you or your sisters and brothers, who were young and liked to enjoy yourselves. You perhaps don't remember how many excuses I had to make up to keep your father from finding out Nené was going out in a *comparsa.* Remember the time Monín, Moña and Nené went to *arrollar*[110] with the one from Paso Franco? We were living in Cristina. Rubiera sent them to bed early and they went out the back door; and when the conga line went past the door of our house, your dad was leaning out the window; the kids had bandanas covering their faces and when they went by him, Monín tweaked his nose, and he shouted indignantly:

– Go screw your mother, you black bastard!

How was he to know it was his own son! The next day we had a big laugh about that.

After I explained and explained that you were young and had the right to enjoy yourselves, one year he brought a truck from the transport company and told you to decorate it, that he was going to take us out carnivalling. That's what they used to do: decorated trucks and carts would parade through the streets where the *fiestas* were. We were so excited! We did the truck up so nicely, decorated it with palm leaves, coloured paper, and put two big benches in it. When it got dark, we all got in. Rubiera had invited my mama and she'd accepted, so we went to pick up Isabel. … What he did to us was unpardonable: he drove the truck through the darkest, loneliest streets of Santiago. I did not forgive him; I felt so sorry for my mama and all of you and for myself. Because of that, I started giving you permission to go out behind his back, to go to the pictures, dancing, and later wherever. With the boys I didn't have to, they just took off and I looked the other way.

Now I dance on my birthday – and any other occasion that might arise – I choose some music to put on, what's popular, and I dance a little with my children and grandchildren. We have a great time. And when I remember, we grab each other around the waist and sing, *Iyá, la panza; panza Iyá*. This year – 1996 – I chose some music from what you lot call the *Hit Parade:* a *son* by Adalberto Alvarez called *El toca toca*. I danced with my grandson Kiko, while the rest of my family, friends and neighbours gathered round singing. I really, really enjoyed that! My sister Gloria was here too. They went to pick her up at her house in the afternoon and that made me very, very happy as well.

When your nephew, Anselmo, came back from abroad, not long ago, his ship docked here, in Santiago; he came to see me straight away and said to Tata:

– Get my grandmother dressed for me.

– What for? Where are you going to take her?

– For a walk.

He took me to a tourist restaurant here in Santiago, called Miguel Matamoros. We ate there and had a few drinks, I wanted to sing with one of the guitarists and I did. It seems I attracted the attention of some Americans who were there; they were talking about me in their language and I answered them – I understand a bit of that language – so they came and sat at our table. They were astonished to see someone of my age so well-disposed and cheerful; we had a great time. At about midnight, I said to my grandson:

– Take me home, I think I'm drunk now.

When we got there, your sister was ready to kill; she insulted Anselmo a thousand ways and he just answered:

– Oh, auntie! That was just an injection of life for my grandma, so she'll still be here when I come back.

'Macuní suncí, macuní sunzá'

I used to love to sing. I was always singing. For about fifteen years now I've hardly sung at all, since your son died in that accident: it's one of those things, a sadness... Sometimes I frighten myself when I sing, it seems like I'm doing something bad. There are things that get impressed on your soul – and I'm a good singer!

Two of my cousins were *trovadores*, sometimes they'd come to my house and sing. I love the traditional *trova* ballads, I like the new ones too; for me the lyrics of the old ones were better than the ones now, more romantic, more sentimental. I loved Carlos Gardel's tangos.[111] I always sang one called *Silencio en la noche*, which was my favourite.

In the first twenty years of the Republic, when they opened a new business or factory, they would go through the streets with loudspeakers announcing it. I remember a song they did for the 'Bacardi' rum factory, that went:

From the factories of the East
Comes a lovely smell
As Cuba's special magic
Weaves its crazy spell
And offers man his potion
From valleys to the ocean
His pain it disguises
Like an eastern sun it rises
Bacardi Rum, Bacardi Rum
In a crystal glass you come
Dead bodies you restore
Deepest sorrow you cure
The world's best for sure.

I loved singing all of you – and later my grandchildren – to sleep; that's why I had such a big repertoire which, along with my daughters, my daughters-in-law and granddaughters inherited and use like I did. My favourite was *Macuní suncí, mancuní sunzá*:

Macuní suncí, mancuní sunzá,
give me the ring,
give me the ring,
you're wearing on your hand.
If you don't give it to me,
if you don't give it to me,
I'll burst into tears.

You liked *Don Tribilín*. Remember how it went? I haven't forgotten, it was:

I am don Tribilín, at your service,
I almost never get any rest;
I go out on the street, I go out once again,
I throw myself off balconies, I break my bowler hat,
I haven't got a cent, I am completely skint,
when I go to the park, they will often say
don Tribilín has a violin,
when he plays it, fuin, fuin, fuin.

I know lots of beautiful lullabies and other funny ones. Modern mothers don't seem to sing to their children. The majority of children these days are distracted by television.

The path to history

When Batista's dictatorship fell, in 1959, the reunion with my sons was a tremendous joy. On 2nd January, after giving thanks to the Virgin of Charity of El Cobre for bringing them back to me alive, we left for Bayamo in a truck they lent your dad from the transport company where he worked. There we met the boys. How handsome they were! With their olive green uniforms and their long hair and beards; one, with officer rank. They were an honour to the *Mambí* tradition of my ancestors and my father. We spent a couple of days with them, then they had to go on to Havana.

In Santiago, I joined the Revolution: the Defence Committee, the Federation of Cuban Women,[112] the National Revolutionary Militia. You enrolled at the university, I was so happy! – finally, one of my children had this opportunity, even if it was only one.

Fate had a rough blow reserved for me. Yankee imperialism perpetrated yet another sabotage against the revolution: the explosion of the ship *La Coubre*.[113] They started broadcasting the casualty information on the radio, that was so awful, everyone was remorseful and indignant.

Rubiera got back from Bayamo that night with the news that Monín had been on the dock when the ship exploded and was injured. Oh, my God, my son! I wanted to go to Havana but there was no way to get there: the airport was closed, there were no flights, it was all in the hands of the army. I spent the whole night worrying, without closing my eyes... I was terrified. The next day, very early in the morning, I was standing in the doorway looking out at the street, when I saw your sister Moña come round the corner, practically running. When she got to me, all teary-eyed, she hugged me hard, very hard... I didn't need words. I said to her:

– He's dead, isn't he?

– Yes mama, I heard it on this morning's report on *Radio Reloj*.

I didn't want to have to talk about this... but since you say it's necessary, I'll make an effort... They're my memories... right? What came next was as difficult as his death: our television was broken, I wanted to see the whole thing, everything they broadcast. Relatives and friends started arriving as they found out. Elsa, our neighbour from across the street, offered me her house to watch the television, it was like a funeral home... people arrived with bouquets of flowers... I don't know who put out a big washtub with water, and they put them in there.

It was like a wake... Us, all his relatives and friends... And the coffin... on the television screen! Oh my God! My son! Why do you make me talk about this?... I suffered so much... His wife Elsa was by my side – pregnant – and at my feet were his two little children, Carlitos and Conchita. And, to add to our pain, every time the camera focussed on the coffin, my son Nené, alone, with no other family member to share this enormous grief.

They called Nené in Bayamo – where he was working – to come and identify the body. Since your dad was there, he said to him: 'Pancho, they've told me Monín is injured, you go to Santiago, I'm going straight to Havana.'

He didn't want to tell him he was dead, not knowing how he would react; he was also worried about how the old man would give me the news. Nené drove like a maniac to Camagüey and caught a military plane there which took him to Havana.

That was so awful, I can still remember, down to the last detail, the voice of Pinelli[114] reporting... The streets like a carpet of flowers for the funeral cars to pass over, all the people in the street, the funeral oration... Fidel spoke with such sorrow and such steadfastness!... I don't know how I stood it... My son was gone!

Five days later Elsa gave birth. It was a boy, a gift from the Virgin; she took one away, the one I'd asked her to lend me, but she sent me another! So we gave him his father's name: Anselmo! His birth woke me out of the lethargy I'd fallen into: there were his children, they had to be raised, to grow up to be men and a woman, to do what he no longer could. I had to help his wife as well, that girl whom life had dealt such a cruel blow.

I revived a little, suffering on the inside. These sorrows never disappear as you know, because you lost a son too. There was still my meeting with Nené... Why didn't he come?... What was taking him so long?... My poor son! I knew he was trying to gather strength to confront me, looking for arguments to explain to me his brother's death... In his terrible grief, he didn't notice, not then nor later, that the whole thing had been televised. He thought I didn't know anything.

The day he arrived, I happened to be the one to open the door when he knocked. It was him... We looked at each other in silence... Dry eyed. I felt the need to protect him from any more suffering and all I said was:

– You lost your comrade!

That was so hard... so hard for him, that he arrived in Santiago with grey hair; he went grey from one day to the next. But it strengthened him, it really made him stronger, to such an extent that two years later he went to Havana, took out his brother's remains and brought them here. He came back with that coffin by his side, right up against his body for the whole journey, which was made even longer because he had to drive... When he arrived he told me: 'Mama, Monín's here now, close to us, I just took him to Santa Ifigenia.[115] Now you can go take him flowers!' All that marked your brother Nené very deeply.

I had asked my *Virgencita* to lend Monín to me and she had granted my request, saving him as an infant. And when she took him, she did it in the best possible way, he went into history! Because – as our national anthem says – *'to die for the country is to live'* because, although he fell there, he is here, in our hearts, because for us, Monín is still alive!

Chapter 4

Me.
Just me. Wilful
woman. As much have I of life
as I asked for. She's given me everything.
Tremendous strength
from then until now.
No storm has blown over
my trunk, nor exposed my roots to the air.
My branches? There they are:
multiplied, flowering.
Fountain of love and life
am I

Earning my way

When I was first married I was quite obedient to my husband.
He was a very fussy eater: I had to get up much earlier, because
he had fried eggs, rice and a glass of Sansón wine for breakfast.
As well as that, when I woke him up I put his socks on and laid
out his underpants and trousers so he just had to step out of
bed and into his shoes, pull up his pants and button them up.
He didn't demand it of me, I did it willingly and for a long
time.

Your dad didn't allow me to develop myself the way I wanted,
to struggle to fulfil the ambitions you all had. I couldn't do it,
Rubiera wouldn't let me; he loved all of you very much, he
never looked down on you, but he never shared the aspirations
I had. I wanted you all to be something in life.

He wanted you to be decent, honest and hard-working. But when he said 'put them to work', what did he mean? Wash, iron, carry sacks, eh, that I did not want! I didn't want my children working in the streets at such a young age, much less as anyone's servants. I wanted to see you progress, not to be *just anyone*. That was my dream and I had to strive for it.

As my children grew and started leaning out into life and finding out about existence, I battled for them to get ahead. But Rubiera wouldn't let me, thinking a woman had to dedicate herself to running the household and nothing more. So I sacrificed everything, I sacrificed myself as a woman to be just a mother, I had to break with tradition and begin to struggle alone.

That's why I separated from Rubiera. No! I didn't *fight* with him, I started building a life independent of your dad in order to be able – off my own back – to give all of you what I yearned for: an education, personal development, minding the atmosphere in which you'd grow up, keep you away from the difficult aspects of life. You know? I couldn't be happy at the cost of your happiness, and raising and educating you was to help you become free men and women. But Rubiera didn't have these criteria.

I was the only one who knew what went on inside the house; I made sure no one found out about my worries and wants. I never went hungry, but I did suffer from a lack of affection and stimulation; I couldn't achieve something I always desired: to go out walking with my husband and children, I never had that pleasure and it would have been so wonderful!

Because of all that, I felt the need to be an independent person and devoted myself to working – something I always enjoyed – to earn my way, not depend on anyone, which meant being free: economic independence is the only way to be free. Since I wasn't the kind of person who could earn a living in an office or in any kind of job other than servant – and that, I was not willing to do – I was always coming up with work I could do in my house.

I began by starting up a *tren de cantinas*.[116] The son of the owner of *Expreso Velar* married a woman who didn't know how to cook; he suggested I make their meals for them and she found the food so delicious and went round telling everyone what a good cook I was, she was free advertising for me. People started coming to my house and gradually I started getting customers: teachers, office workers and, especially, prostitutes. I eventually had twenty-one *cantinas*; I bought them in instalments, paying them off little by little, as the business prospered. Your dad, who had always given me a small allowance for daily expenses, stopped it when I established the *tren de cantinas*.

I also washed and ironed *guayaberas*[117] and white suits. I washed clothes for a lot of people who liked to be well-dressed and weren't satisfied with the job the laundry did, so I got more customers and I made a little money. There was a time when I sold coal, eggs and even perfume; the latter I got from an Arab gentleman who had a warehouse of perfumes, talcum powder, soap and things like that. I remember the bottles of *Reuter's* toilet-water and *Pompeya* perfume. He'd give me the products, I'd sell them and keep a certain percentage.

In spite of everything I couldn't pay cash for the things I needed: I had a lot of children and no choice other than to buy in instalments; because you could buy what you needed without being limited by the money you had. Every time I got something I felt very satisfied. One time I was standing in the doorway with your sister Pura when a girl went by and said: 'Oh, how pretty! All covered in blue. Oh, if only I could have shoes like those!' For me it was very satisfying, because I worked to cover the needs of my household. But I reached that conclusion when – for material and spiritual reasons – I had electricity installed.

I swear I'll buy a radio!

At the beginning of the 1940s – you were just a tiny baby – we were still using kerosene to light the house. This was normal, to a certain extent: there were lots of poor families who didn't have electric lights in their houses. I loved the soap operas on the radio; at that time there was one with María Valero and Ernesto Galindo,[118] the most famous romantic couple of the day. My next door neighbours had a radio in their kitchen and the wall between our houses was wooden; so I'd press my ear to the wall when my neighbour turned it on. The day the soap was at its emotional height, they moved the radio from where it had been, maybe they realized I was listening – because they were nasty. I don't know if it was sadness or indignation, but at that very instant I swore I'd buy a radio!

The first thing I had to do was get my house wired for electricity. I didn't consult with your dad; I made inquiries, found the money and had electricity installed! *Ay, muchacha!* What a day that was! I wouldn't let them turn on the one light bulb we had put in the middle of the living room, until it got dark. Rubiera watched us without saying a word, he didn't know whether to approve or not of what was going on. How exciting when the time finally came to light it; all my children around me and when we turned it on, what joy! So much that your brother Monín – who was almost a young man by then – stood at attention and sang the *National Anthem*. Funny, eh? But if you think about it, sad, very sad.

The next day your sister Moña and I went to a shop to look at radios. They sold them on instalment plans and you could keep it for a week's trial period, if for any reason it wasn't suitable, you could take it back. After getting the electricity installed I didn't have enough money for a down payment on a radio; it occurred to me to order one of any brand to have for a trial period, take it back after a week and go to another store to try one of some other brand. So I spent a time listening to radios on approval until I saved enough money for a down-payment to buy my own.

I haven't forgotten, it was a *Firestone*. Now I had electricity and a radio! That episode caused an important transformation in me, a big change had occurred in my life: my independence! After that I could do things without telling the old man, I'd broken the tradition of submission to the man of the house. To such an extent that one time when your dad sat down to listen to another programme at the time the soap opera was on, I said to him:

– *Ay chico*, let me listen to the soap, it's really good.

– Bah, Mima, get over your romanticism!

That really bothered me because he enjoyed electric light and the radio as if he'd always had them, so I said:

– No, Rubiera, it's my radio! I bought the radio.

And I picked it up, and took it into the kitchen to listen to the soap.

After that I devoted myself to working with even more determination: as well as the take-away, I set up a little dining room in my house, my living room was quite spacious, during the day I moved my furniture against the wall and had two tables with four chairs around each – the neighbourhood carpenter made them for me and I paid him for them bit by bit. I put tablecloths on and served my customers there. Everything I needed for my little diner I bought in instalments. Don't go thinking it was anything elegant, but it was very clean.

It was humble people who ate there: dock-workers, street vendors and occasionally someone just passing by at mealtime. I didn't charge a lot; things were very difficult then, there were lots of men out of work, a lot of poverty, misery. I didn't earn much money, but it was something to help you get ahead.

I would finish at night, rather late. Just think of it! Cook, attend anyone who arrived and afterwards the washing up! *Ay, mi madre!* The dishes to wash! Your older sisters helped me, but I didn't like to leave the whole mess to them because there was also your dad and you bunch to look after. When I finished and went to lie down, what fell into bed was a lead weight, but most nights I couldn't go to sleep right away because Rubiera would take a fancy and...

The living room suite

In 1949 or 1950 we moved to Cristina Street by Gasómetro, and once again I had decisions to make. We had a small, tatty set of furniture and the old rocking chairs; the house was a good one, big and pretty, with a living room and parlour, remember how ugly it looked with the old furniture? I had to buy a new living room suite. I mentioned it to Moña, that one's a character! The next day when she came back from her classes she said to me:

– Mama, I went by the *Barrios* furniture shop and saw a big beautiful living room suite. They sell on instalment plans.

The next day we both went and bought it; and as if that weren't enough, we also bought a couple of pictures, a vase and crêpe paper flowers, also on instalment. We set up the house, it looked so pretty! When Rubiera got home he had a fit and said:

– María, you're crazy! Don't count on me to pay for this.

His words didn't bother me. Remember what Moña did the next day? Well, she went to school – she wanted all her friends to see the new furniture – and had the idea of pretending to faint. So the teachers told several of her friends to take her home; she arrived all weak and dizzy and threw herself on the sofa – which was very big – with one eye closed and the other open, to watch her friend's faces as they saw the house looking so pretty.

Moña was always doing things like that. But her pride in having an attractive, tidy house, the satisfaction you all showed, was my prize for all that effort, it was what gave me incentive to keep struggling. But without separating from Rubiera; my children had to grow up with their mama and their dad, that's very important.

In that house I was able to give you another pleasure, because all of you were always wanting to have a Christmas tree and we'd never been able to buy one. I put up a big tree with balls and decorations and little coloured lights that went on and off. We also made a nativity scene. The boys made mountains out of empty cement sacks; we made straw from unravelled and dyed rope; and we bought the figures. We made a little lake out of a piece of a mirror and put ducks on it and animals around it. It was lovely!

You were all happy. Me? Of course, I was happy too! Things were starting to go the way I wanted. That year the whole family was together, we celebrated Christmas Eve, the old man ate with us and, for the first time in my life, I got drunk. I wasn't used to alcoholic drinks, so after a couple, I was tipsy. It was a double intoxication: on rum and happiness.

And I bought a fridge

I was determined to solve all the problems of my household and I thought I'd better buy myself a fridge, but I couldn't decide. On various occasions I'd said to Rubiera:

– *Viejo*, don't you think it's time we got a fridge?

– Mima, are you crazy? You think I'm rich or something?

As an answer your dad himself made an 'icebox'. He got a wooden box with a lid and lined it with zinc. Around the box and the lid he put a seal made out of strips of an inner tube from a truck, so it wouldn't let the cold out. An ice vendor went by the house and we'd buy from him and put it in the 'icebox', and we'd put the water bottles and whatever else in there. I already told you I was used to shopping every day. The problem was that the ice vendor didn't always come by and then there wouldn't be any cold water. I was getting tired of the situation.

One really hot day when there was no ice – and that happened often – I sent a little neighbour to another neighbour's house to ask her to send me a glass of cold water. When the little girl came back she said: 'María, she says, why don't you buy ice, why are you always bothering her.' It was more than enough: the next day I went to resolve that problem.

When I went to buy the fridge, I had no money. I received a pension that... Oh, dear! I don't know if I'll ever be brave enough to tell you what I found out because of it... Well, I went to a store and chose one. The sales assistant told me what I'd need to put down as a deposit and how much the monthly payments would be. I talked to him, I can't remember how much I told him, but I convinced him to let me take the fridge, leaving my pension papers as a guarantee, and that the following month I'd bring the down payment and the first instalment. And he gave it to me!

I went to find a truck belonging to a friend of Rubiera's, who, of course, was insulted and said:

– You're crazy! This won't last a month here. How are we going to pay for it?

I didn't pay any attention to what he said and set a plan to achieve my objective. The next day I bought fruit and started making popsicles; I made ice, fruit drinks, *pru*, all for sale. It went well, almost none of the neighbours had refrigerators. We were living in 'Luis Dagnesse' then, a very poor neighbourhood. I bought a money-box and after thirty days I had enough for the down-payment and the electricity.

What tragedies from you bunch! Never happy with only one popsicle or a little drink, you wanted to keep up with the customers. I made the monthly payments from my pension and paid the electricity bill from what I sold. So I had a refrigerator. There it is! I think it'll last a few years yet. It's a *Crosley* and has served me well, I've had it for forty-four or forty-five years and it's only broken twice.

A few years later I bought a television. But things were different by then, your brothers were working and helped me out with things like that even though they didn't live with me... Oh! To think I even came to have a motor car!

It was a gift from your brothers, the first Mothers' Day after the war ended. They brought it to me from Havana. See the kind of thing your dad did to me! I spoke to a neighbour so he could work it, he'd give me a percentage of what he earned and he'd be responsible for the maintenance. Your dad didn't agree, we argued about it several times. I don't know if he felt inferior because the idea occurred to me and not to him, because it injured his manliness, or out of machismo. The fact is, one day he came home on foot and when I asked him about the motor car he put his hand in his pocket and threw a roll of bills down on the table in front of me. There was no need for words. He sold my motor car! I blew up, I don't know how I contained myself. I wanted to kill him!

The satin dress

The economic possibilities I started acquiring with all the various jobs I did allowed me to give myself a few pleasures. For me, meeting all the needs of my household, instead of a problem, was a satisfaction: seeing my children well-dressed, well-shod, celebrating your birthdays and, in particular, the

149

weddings of my daughters. For your sister Pura's wedding, I couldn't meet the costs in cash. There was a gentleman called Rafael who would give you a voucher and you'd go to the shop where he had credit and buy the clothes you wanted, and he'd add on a certain percentage and work out the monthly payments you had to make.

That's how I managed to get Pura fitted out for her wedding. Everything we needed for the reception I paid for with the money I'd saved up from my various odd jobs, like holding raffles for bedspreads, tablecloths and dress-lengths. Well, I saved that money and bit by bit, I eventually had enough for the reception. The wedding day arrived: your sister was so beautiful in her gown and train with six bridesmaids. They sang *Ave María* in the church. It was so moving! She was married in the 'Don Bosco' church.

I thought I was in heaven that day, that I was dreaming. Your grandmother and your uncles and aunts were there too. Isabel was proud because Pura's husband was white. I didn't ask the Virgin for that, they met and fell in love. I didn't intervene in any of your choices of partners. I always advised on the qualities to look for in a person: to guarantee happiness, you need calmness and stability as well as love.

Later came Moña's wedding. She was forever leafing through fashion magazines, looking at wedding gowns. At that time they were using satin materials decorated with lace. Moña wanted a satin dress! I didn't think twice about obliging her, went to find Rafael and got into debt again! I bought some white satin and lace, and another material they call *palm shadow* for her going away dress.

I'll never forget the 9th of May 1953. At nine o'clock in the morning they were married in the office of the notary, Dr. Mario Norma. And at six in the evening, once again, the sound of the organ and voices of the choir of the 'Don Bosco' Church singing *Ave María* filled my heart with emotion and joy. It was all just lovely... But we didn't have enough money for a photographer!

My daughter knew but she had a novelist's imagination. The house was full of guests and it was very hot. Moña was embarrassed in front of her friends because there weren't going to be any photos and, to cover up, started saying: 'What's keeping the photographer, it's so hot and I really want to get out of this dress.' Suddenly, as she was already sweating, she said: 'Oh, I feel so dizzy!' and she fainted. They picked her up and carried her to a bed, she whispered in my ear: 'Don't worry, mama, there's nothing wrong with me.' A few minutes later she started to 'come round', and everyone forgot all about the photographer; Moña changed her clothes and went off on her honeymoon. When she came back, we had a portrait taken in a photography studio in her satin dress.

Rubiera didn't participate in the weddings of any of his daughters nor in those of his sons either. Your dad thought poor people shouldn't give themselves such luxuries, that I was getting myself mixed up in these messes because I was getting proud. His criticisms didn't matter to me, though it hurt because what mattered was the happiness of my children, even if I got up to my eyeballs in debt for it.

Luisa, my great friend

Friendship is a profound feeling sustained through comprehension, unselfishness and sincerity, that strengthens with time as we are able to put up with the virtues and defects of the person we call our friend. Because no one's perfect and we can't aspire to find the perfect friendship; perfection does not exist. What we can do is try to be better every day, perfect our way of being, and that's the way we have to see others.

Life is always changing, you might be my friend one day and not the next. Not because there're problems between us, but because we both change. And what unites me with you today might separate me from you tomorrow. For friendship to work it has to be reciprocal, right?

I had one true friend. Her name was Luisa, she was from Cueto; she'd had bad luck as a young girl and because of these tricks of fate she fell into a life of vice; but she was good. And God rewarded her. She met a good man and he married her.

They lived next door to me; their house was very nice, white painted wood with red roof tiles and a little garden always growing flowers. We both enjoyed everything to do with plants, we exchanged cuttings of the different flowers we had, although she preferred ornamental plants and I liked flowers better.

After she got married, Luisa made children's and women's clothing for a living, she sewed very well. It was she who taught me, she was very patient with me. She'd say: 'Reyita, you have to learn to sew, that way you won't have to pay a seamstress and you can dress your children better.'

She was white, not very tall, with very fine skin, lots of curly black hair, her hands and feet used to make me laugh because they were so tiny. She almost always wore white, knee-length dresses with a flounce and decorated with embroidered strips. Her personal cleanliness and the whiteness of her clothes made her stand out, she had a cheerful and contagious smile. She had three children: two girls and a boy.

She became quite well-known as a dressmaker. She also embroidered, did hemming, and beautiful latticework.[119] She didn't charge high prices for her work because, as she put it: 'Poor people have the right to dress nicely too.' I can see her now, sitting at her sewing machine, or on the front porch of her house, sitting in her rocking chair while she embroidered in the afternoons. Sometimes we'd sit together doing needlework and talking, she would tell me stories of Mayarí, which was her village; she'd tell me about her family, which she'd had to distance herself from because of the life she'd led before getting married. Friendship with her was good, sincere and very reciprocal.

Alms from thieves

Respect for others, decency, knowing how to maintain one's composure in front of life and other people, being a discreet and modest person and not being shameless are what I think one needs in order to call themselves honest; I believe I possess these qualities. Many years ago, something happened to me that I'm not embarrassed by nor am I ashamed to tell you, because I've never made use of anything belonging to anyone else, I never took anything from anyone. And on the occasion that I'm about to describe I was, and still am, sure it was the Virgin, the *Virgencita* of Charity of El Cobre, in whom I have so much faith, who guided me, who helped me and gave me succour.

I was undergoing some pretty bad economic troubles at that time, when I lived in Cueto. One day I woke up very sad and knelt down embracing my *Virgencita*, asking her not to forsake me, to help me one more time. I was also sad that day because I couldn't take your brothers to a circus that was in town. That night, since your dad was on the railway and almost everyone was at the show, I went to the house of the owners of a clothing store – he was called Abraham Cairú – to take a cutting from a lovely climbing lilac bush, because I'd asked Doña Amalia – Cairú's wife – and she had said no.

When I got to the front of the store, what a surprise I found: it was open! I went in. Judging by the mess, I realized it had been robbed, and I thought it must have been the *Virgencita* who had guided my steps this way; I didn't think twice about it, since I only had to cross the street and the front yard of my house, I made three trips. I took a piece of *Rica* material, two

153

or three bedspreads, spools of lace, ribbons; in short, everything
I needed to partially cover the needs of my household. I packed
everything away and lay down to pray, my heart felt like it was
going to burst through my chest; and just like that, hugging
my *Virgencita*, I fell asleep. When your dad got home, he woke
me up:

　　　– Mima, mima, wake up! They robbed Cairú's store.

　　I bolted up in bed, my heart could barely keep beating:

　　　– I went to bed early and didn't hear anything. Did they
take much? Did they catch the thieves?

　　　– I don't know, they say they emptied the store. No one
knows anything about the thieves.

　　I felt a terrible jolt in the pit of my stomach, but hearing
that calmed me down a bit. In the end, what the thieves did
was open the door and leave alms for me. I went back to bed,
thinking how uneven the world was, some with so much, others
with little or nothing. The last thing I remember were the words
of my friend Marcelina a few years before: 'Mistress of what?
Simply Reyita!' Time went by, and due to problems Rubiera
had at work I already told you about – for he didn't like things
done badly – he asked for a transfer to Bayamo, but within the
same company. We moved and there I was able to use all the
things the thieves of Cairú's store had left for me.

Happiness... I got some

There are many ways to be happy: some feel happy because
they have lots of material goods; others because they love and
are loved. There are those who are happy because in their family
no one suffers from headaches or lacks the basic essentials. There
is no better mood than how you feel when you've done a good
deed, or when you can give pleasure, obtain something much
desired. For me all this is happiness. But, I repeat, there are
many ways to feel happy.

Sometimes very high prices must be paid to achieve it because, unfortunately, it's not a permanent condition, it's just from time to time. So you have to know how to take advantage of those instants and enjoy them. Moments of happiness one has had over a lifetime help to overcome the bitter ones, which in some cases are more frequent, but I am convinced that happiness can be constructed.

You need to prepare the conditions so these moments will have more weight than the bitter ones, because these are inevitable, the others we have to cultivate. I was a very poor woman, but I always tried, in the middle of that poverty, to create a joyful and happy atmosphere for all of you. But don't worry, I too had my moments of happiness.

As a little girl, since I had no toys, I made dolls for myself – as I already told you – and I was happy, very happy making them their little clothes, brushing their corn-silk hair, talking to them. I was happy when I was a teacher, in Báguanos. My work gave me that happiness. Despite all my struggles – even though I couldn't actually bring it to fruition – to get into the Institute, I was happy then too, because I found out that I was intelligent and could have done.

I felt happy sharing with my neighbours, when we were sweating in the fields collecting cane, or in the coffee-threshing campaign, working voluntarily after the revolutionary triumph or when I snuck out of the house and went on my own to see a Carlos Gardel or Libertad Lamarque[120] film. You see what I mean? These were moments of happiness I obtained for myself, like those I had trying to make you and my grandchildren happy.

I had a very big *macaco coco*[121] shrub. At night I'd scratch around the roots a little and 'plant' four or five *medios*. In the morning, I'd tell the boys: 'Whoever cleans the yard, the *macaco coco* bush will reward with *medios*. They'd grab up the broom and the hoe and clean up the garden, when they finished they'd scrape around under the bush and find the *medios*. They'd be so pleased! Don't you think that counts as happiness?

Finding myself surrounded by grandchildren during school holidays, singing to them, telling them stories, offering them my home-made candies, teaching them to love one another: That's happiness too. Even after so many years, when one of them wants something outside of his or her real possibilities, and another tells them: 'Be careful, you don't want to end up like Masica,'[122] remembering the character from a story I used to tell them, it makes me feel happy.

Of one thing I am certain. And that's if a person has no love in his heart, he'll never be happy; nor will an egotist, a *casasolo*,[123] nor an overly ambitious person. These defects are incompatible with happiness.

My house!

I've lived in this neighbourhood for thirty-five years. It's relatively new, built after the triumph of the revolution. They gave me the house for being the mother of a martyr; it's a very nice neighbourhood. It's called '30th of November' after some historical event.[124] Almost all the houses look alike, they're spacious and have big gardens. It seems as if they'd made it especially for me, I still enjoy gardening. I believe the Virgin had a lot to do with me having my very own house.

It was right here I had to do something that's always weighed on me. You know I had the picture of the Virgin on the wall facing the street, but when your niece María Elena became a Party member, one day she came home – she lived with me – and said: 'Grandma, I want you to take that image out of the living room. We don't believe in that and it embarrasses me when my comrades come over and see it there. Why don't you put it in your bedroom?'

I still have as much faith in the Virgin as ever. But, times change, I understood my granddaughter's feelings and put it in my room. You can see it from the living room but it's in the old woman's room, 'who can't be expected to change her way of thinking now', as they say. I know it's not pretty, and even quite faded. It's almost three quarters of a century old! But I never wanted to change her because this is the one I've asked things of all my life.

In this house I've had more happy moments than sad ones. Here I saw you graduate from university; this has been the place where almost all my grandchildren have chosen to be married; it was where we celebrated the homecoming of my son Nené, my granddaughter Chabela and other grandchildren when they got back from their internationalist missions in Africa, where they fulfilled a double duty, one of solidarity and one they indirectly had to the land of my grandmother.

Yes, I've had many happy moments in this house. And as a postscript, the marvellous days with the comrades who came to make a video,[125] in which I was the main character. The star! They were very busy days which I really enjoyed because, even though I'm ninety-four you know I've still got all my marbles and I don't want to be a neglected, useless, old woman who can't manage by herself, who can't function. I've always tried to do something useful, always been ready to help and accompany my children. That's worth a lot! Since I prefer helping others to being helped, I keep working.

Of all the things I learned in my youth, knitting is what lets me earn a living nowadays. I knit a lot: table covers, handkerchiefs, children's socks, and this money lets me help, not my children anymore but my grandchildren. You know I have to knit like a spider because between grandchildren, great-grandchildren, and great-great-grandchildren, I've got more than a hundred. And so, when I see them with some need, I can give myself the satisfaction of helping them! Because my grandchildren mean more to me than you bunch because they're your children. In order to keep struggling for them, I take good care of myself.

My rainbow

I have very strong family values, I sacrificed many things for mine because the times demanded it. I believe the parents – both of them, the father and the mother – have the obligation not only to feed and clothe their children, but to surround them with a caring atmosphere of confidence and respect, to get what one desires out of them, that they may become honest, honourable men, respected by and respecting others, proud of who they are and loving what they do.

Children must be inculcated with a love of their country too; teach them to get along with others. You have to have good, affectionate and polite relationships with them; only in this way, I repeat, can we assure they'll be good people. And I say I've sacrificed myself a lot, because I had to do it all alone. In this sense I had to be mother and father; but it wasn't in vain because I achieved an organized and united family of decent, honourable and strong men and women. I don't have any convicts or vagrants in my family, no drunks or prostitutes, none are abnormal or crippled, and even luckier, they're all in Cuba. Do you realize what we've got?

Now there are one hundred and eighteen of us: eight children, thirty-nine grandchildren, sixty-four great-grand children and seven great-great-grandchildren. Isn't that right? My family's beautiful! It looks like a rainbow: whites, blacks, *mulaticos, jabaítos*. Long hair, short hair, curly and straight. Engineers, lawyers, teachers, technicians, workers; all organized and, most importantly, free of racial prejudices.

One time I went to spend some time at the house of your niece Reyita – it was for New Year – and they held a little party on the 24th of December to which they invited all the parents of their friends. Because we old folks are always hankering for Christmas Eve. The children were fighting over who had the prettiest grandmother, I was the only black one. Carlitín – my great-grandson – stood up and said: 'No one can deny it, my grandma is the prettiest of all.' That made me proud, of course, it was what love made the child see.

We're spread out all over the country: Santiago, Holguín, Matanzas, Havana, Pinar del Río. That doesn't mean I forget any of their birthdays, I take pleasure in each of them receiving a congratulatory telegram I always send on those dates. That's why you all say I unite us, because even if we can't get all one hundred and eighteen of us together for every holiday, all it needs is for me to get the slightest bit ill – and thank God I've got an iron constitution – for everyone to come running.

I've only been in hospital twice in my life because when I gave birth, it was at home with midwives. When they operated on my eyes, to the cry of: 'Grandma's having surgery!' What a mobilization! Everyone came. In the hospital I had contradictory feelings: on the one hand I felt very proud, because my family couldn't fit in the room; and on the other hand, I was embarrassed, there were so many! There was no room for any other patient's visitors.

One night comes to mind when I woke up dying of hunger, I got up quietly, opened the fridge, ate some roast pork rind and a green tomato, drank a glass of water, and went back to bed. Result: the next day they were removing my gall bladder, and it was all: 'hurry, hurry!' I was already in the recovery room when you arrived from Havana. It was very funny when the nurse came in and said: 'Can the patient with the hundred and sixteen relatives get ready, she's going to have an injection.' Am I mistaken? No, my latest great-grandson and great-great-granddaughter hadn't been born yet. I've got the sum right.

159

On my last birthday, your niece Conchita sent me a card from Havana that made me so happy I'm going to read a bit of it:

> Dear Grandma,
>
> ... I've been overwhelmed by all this commotion around you[126] ... The greatness of your soul and your heart, your gentleness and wisdom have borne great fruit in this enormous family that You have forged like a blacksmith, always by the anvil. Everything we are we owe in great measure to You...

That's what I've gained through my struggle and sacrifice. That's my family!

When words sing

I've always been very romantic. As a young girl I loved to read poems, it was one of my hobbies. I had to work so much! I frequently spent my 'spare' time reading poetry. I fell desperately in love with a poet, my favourite: Juan de Dios Peza.[127] He wrote the most lovely things, sometimes I'd close my eyes like this, and imagine he wrote them for me. I knew almost all of them off by heart. I remember a few in their entirety. I'm going to recite a few stanzas of a monologue entitled *Alone:*

> You're going? Farewell! He left at last.
> What a horrible night!
> the city seems calm
> a big empty grave
> and a wind so chill
> like winter in the soul...
> ... And this branch?
> Who presents me with flowers?
> Purple April roses
> have fewer thorns

than I sorrows...

It was very long but so beautiful. Even though Juan de Dios Peza was the one I liked the most, I also loved José Jacinto Milanés.[128] Um! ... *Tórtola mía, Turtle-dove of mine...* And others. There was one by la Avellaneda[129] – I don't remember, let me think – oh, yes, there was a stanza that went:

> *...Blessed may you live! If one day*
> *you see this farewell I send eternal,*
> *know in my soul you still possess*
> *generous forgiveness, fond tenderness.*

It was a bit long, called *A mi amor... A él.* I can't really remember. I read a lot of poems by Luisa Pérez de Zambrana,[130] Amado Nervo.[131] Oh, my dear! If only I had the memory I used to have, I'm starting to lose it. You don't think so? You're just trying to butter me up.

Now they write a kind of poetry which I'm not going to tell you categorically I don't like. What happens is that some don't rhyme and others I don't understand. But, fine, each to his own. For me poetry has its music. Every once in a while I read a book of poems because one thing I still haven't lost is my sensibility.

Love and tenderness

There are many ways of expressing this tremendous emotion one feels for another person. Love is something really beautiful; anyone with love in their heart loves all beauty, not just the external, but what each person or thing carries inside. This feeling doesn't arise of itself, it must be guided, because there are bad loves too, egotistical, sickening, that don't make anyone happy...

There is filial love, carnal love, brotherly love; but they all involve deep tenderness, like I felt for my grandchildren when they were tiny, I loved them so much! Oh, honey, I'm so old now! Sometimes I want to explain things to you and my head gets all chaotic. Now my mind is filled with images of the day they brought Rosa María to the house for me to see her, and Reyita, and Miriam and Moncho, to spend a few days. When they arrived, they all kissed me, except Moncho; I said to him:

– Won't you give your grandma a little kiss?

– No, I don't want to.

– Well, I'm going to die then.

Since he just shrugged his shoulders, I threw myself on the floor and played dead; what an outcry!

– Ay, grandma! Grandma, don't die!

– You see Moncho, it's your fault.

He thought it was true and threw himself on top of me, crying and covering me with kisses. Then I 'came back to life' and my grandchildren were filled with joy.

We are capable of giving up many things for love. Your niece Reyita's husband had some problems with his family – they're white – for marrying her. I was at Pura's house the day he came to ask for her hand in matrimony. And I said to him:

– Have you thought carefully about this? Reyita has white skin, but she's mestiza; marrying her brings you right into little Africa.

– That doesn't matter, I'm marrying her, not the colour of her family.

The tenderness and affection you all feel for me doesn't allow anyone to offend or injure me. Réyima, Reyita's daughter, fell out with her first boyfriend over that. Remember when she brought him to meet me? You were here, he started talking about his Spanish grandparents, how they had some businesses... I don't know what else. She didn't like it and in the end thought this attitude would bring her problems in future familial relations. And she left him.

But if it's carnal love we're dealing with, that's something else. It arises out of a mutual attraction two people feel, out of affinity, out of having something in common; if it comes just out of simple physical attraction, then it's not love. One can fall in love with anything, a lovely pair of eyes, a beautiful body, a nice way of speaking. In this sense I've had many experiences because I've fallen in love many times. To love and to be in love, there are differences there too, don't you think? I can love you but not be in love with you...

When I was very young, there was a man called Enrique Bayard – serious, educated, hard-working. He liked me because, although it's not nice for me to say it, I was a very pretty girl. He went to see Mamacita to tell her he wanted to marry me, he was going to give her four hundred pesos – that was a lot of money then – to get me ready. When my grandmother called me to tell me, I didn't accept, I had nothing in common with him, I didn't love him. Luckily I was living with my grandma in Banes; she didn't even try to convince me because she agreed with me. Enrique Bayard loved me, because he insisted even knowing I didn't love him; because to love is to give everything in exchange for nothing.

I got pregnant by looking at him

My mama washed and ironed the clothes for a family who owned a dairy in La Maya. They paid her with two churns full of milk. She sold one and kept the other for the people in her house. The one who brought the milk was the son of the owner of the dairy. A very handsome, swarthy young man. That man was so good-looking that even at my age I noticed him!

Isabel had a neighbour called Victoria, and her daughter –
who was single – got pregnant. My mama asked her, when
they were talking:

– How did you get so careless?

– No *chica*, they saw each other at the river when she
went to wash. I didn't know anything.

Listening to this conversation I deduced that women got
pregnant by looking at men. So, when he came I looked at
him, I stared at him, I ran my hand over my belly, like this. I
looked at him so insistently that he said: '*Negrita*, what are you
looking at?' And I looked away. After a few months, I told my
mama one day:

– Isabel, I think I'm pregnant.

– How's that, Reyita?

– Yes, Isabel, I'm pregnant now.

– And who are you pregnant by?

– By Alejo.

– And how did you get pregnant by Alejo?

– Because every day when he comes I look at him, and I
look at him and pass my hand over my belly, like this. And
now I'm pregnant just like Victoria's daughter.

Isabel realized I'd overheard that conversation and, dying
of laughter, called Queta, the next-door neighbour, and told
her the story. The two of them started laughing. Watching
them making fun of me I burst into tears and told them:

– You don't believe me, I am pregnant.

My mama explained to me why it was impossible. I didn't
understand anything. I was eight then.

When the train came in

An engineer called Julio Chanton worked on the train that
stopped at La Maya. He was a man who, to my adolescent eyes
of thirteen or fourteen, seemed very gallant. He was tall,

mulatto, strong and very handsome. He wore these blue overalls, very starched and pressed, with a white shirt underneath and a cap with a visor, also blue. He always had a red and white polka-dot bandanna tied around his neck.

I went to the station every day to see him arrive; when I heard *chugga chugga, chugga chugga* and I knew the train was coming in, I'd get terribly nervous. When it was at the platform, the noise of the escaping steam would make my heart leap. I can't tell you how I felt. And when I saw him get down and lean against the train, as if he were tired, wiping off the sweat. *Ay muchacha!* He seemed so important. Just imagine, driving that big train, with all those people. All those lives in his hands. I felt so much admiration for him and so, day after day I'd go to the station to see 'superman' and think: 'If only I could marry a man like him, so strong, so interesting and with such an important job.'

One time I went, as usual, to see him come in. I stopped behind one of the wooden columns that held up the station roof. I'd thought of getting close to him, saying something to him, anything, just so he'd notice me. But what a surprise I got! When he got down, a girl, who was standing almost beside me, ran up to him and they hugged and kissed, he put his arm around her and they walked away entwined together. Chanton, the man I'd built so many hopes around, was spoken for! I ran out of there. I couldn't keep two big fat tears from rolling down my cheeks.

And he looked like Mella[132]

In Cueto there was a tall young man, thin and olive-skinned. He had beautiful black eyes, with a profound and penetrating look. He was very handsome. He was always passing by the door of my dad's house – it was when I lived with him – and I always managed to be there. He greeted me smiling but the intensity of his look made me nervous, made my heart beat faster. After a few months I started to fall in love. I was happy and, for the first time, really in love.

I took great pains in fixing myself up, making myself pretty, doing my hair in fashionable styles – I could afford a few luxuries because I had a fee-paying school and I earned a little money. Just when everything looked set to happen, after he'd finally spoken to me and asked me to become his proper girlfriend, another showed up. She came between us and he decided on her.

That really hurt, it was my first heart-break. It hurt me so much that I started to think all men who came near me were going to do the same. I didn't fall in love again until I met your dad. But listen, honey, I was deeply in love with that young man.

Speaking from the heart

I didn't want a black husband, not out of contempt for my race, but because black men had almost no possibilities of getting ahead and the certainty of facing a lot of discrimination. Their best chance was in sports: being a boxer; giving but also receiving many blows, and with age ending up all disfigured and traumatized, you know?

For this reason, out of all the poems I read, the one I never liked was that one called *Go to sleep little black boy,*[133] or something like that, because in it were reflected – according to its author – the highest aspirations of a black man, or that a black mother could have for her son. One of the lines goes: '*When you get big you're gonna be a boxer...*' uh, only we know what our real aspirations are. But anyway, apart from that, if a black man dreamed of getting away from poverty, back then, he had to set himself up as a huckster or a thug, and in the end, what? The penitentiary or death, and the reformatory for the younger ones.

And a black woman didn't have a less unsettled destiny: Work as a servant, laundress, or fall into prostitution, to end up in the hospital or the penitentiary, if she hadn't already taken the turn-off for the cemetery. This is what I didn't want for the children I was going to have. That's why I asked my *Virgencita* for a white husband. I wouldn't have been able to put up with seeing my children humiliated, harassed, mistreated, and much less living a life of vice. That's why I married a white man.

When I met your dad and realized he liked me, I didn't give in to him easily – in those days they used to say women 'went' with their boyfriends. No, I wouldn't accept that. I wanted to marry as God meant me to, and I lay down this condition: 'If you want me to be your woman, you have to marry me.' During the short time he was courting me I came to love him. Sometimes I think it was love out of gratitude, but I loved him; he obliged and married me.

How was our love life? What you would expect between two people in love. He got into the habit of whistling for me when he was getting close to home after work, and I'd wait for him at the door, all clean and neat and smelling nice. We'd hug and kiss. It was always like that for the first ten or fifteen years of our married life. I told you I was very romantic, that I'd read lots of love stories and I liked him to be bold in our sexual relations.

At first he wanted to make love with the light on. I wouldn't let him, not because I didn't like it but because I was embarrassed; but I did understand it was a nuisance to undress in the dark with all the clothing we used to wear back then. Another of his struggles was to see me naked. He had a job of it, but he managed. Later we even bathed together, we even made love in the bath! And I'm not going to deny that I liked it. Well, we got so comfortable with each other we even had sexual relations in the truck – when we went to the beach. I'm telling you very intimate things about my private life, but I did so many things to please your dad... *Ay muchacha!* Heh, heh, heh. I always loved ribbons. I always wore them and in some flight of amorous madness I put them in my hair, and not just on my head...!

There was a stage when Rubiera got a bit brusque. I thought he was having an affair, but no, he went to the doctor and got prescribed some injections called *Primotex*. He had one each week. Everything went back to normal. But then he got the hernia, and 'it' grew, and I don't know what it was, just thinking about that big 'sack'. I never even looked at it. That's why we stopped making love a few years before he died.

I loved the old man a lot, but I was never in love with him. My true love was the first one, the one who looked like Mella, who I remember each time I see a photo of that revolutionary in a newspaper, magazine or on the television. I'm going to confess something to you that I've always kept guarded in the bottom of my heart. Many times, making love with your dad, I'd close my eyes, let my imagination fly, until it seemed I was with him, the one who looked like Mella. That's infidelity too, although not realized. Why haven't I told you his name? Forgive me, but let me keep it to myself.

After 1951 or 1952, I can't remember exactly, when my dad died, in the toings and froings around my pension as a daughter of a veteran, a notary – your sister Carlota's godfather – went to do I don't know what, to see if I could qualify – because I was married – and he got a copy of my birth certificate. When he went to get a copy of my marriage licence, a great truth came to light. I was single!

– No, it can't be.

I said to Coloma, the notary.

– Yes, Reyita, you're single.

– There must be a mistake.

– No, there's not. You were never married.

– What's this? My God! Why has Rubiera done this to me?

And I remembered that day, back in Cueto. The hotel reception room all decorated, the flowers, the cake. Me wearing a simple knee-length white dress, a gift from Señora Muñoz, with my hair done in such a pretty way with flowers over the top. Rubiera elegantly dressed, the notary – he wasn't improvised – he was the town notary; Muñoz, his wife; Carderrosa, his wife.

– Señorita María de los Reyes Castillo Bueno, do you take Señor Antonio Amador Rubiera Gómez to be your husband...?

– I do.

– Señor Antonio Amador Rubiera...

– I do.

– I now pronounce you husband and wife.

False, all false! Was everyone involved in this compound lie? Or just Rubiera and the notary? But, why? Dear God, why? I felt as if my mind were shrinking or getting tangled, I couldn't think. Why this deceit? It didn't make sense, he was with me, with all of you. I felt a huge pain in my heart. What to do? Reproach him? Demand he tell me why he did it?

I spent several days unable to think straight. Later I thought and thought, and decided what to do. I followed all the procedures for obtaining the veteran's pension; meanwhile, I avoided him and kept away from him using any excuse. When they sent me the papers for the pension, I showed them to him – to see his reaction. He went red, he wanted to say something, but I didn't let him. That was his punishment, to carry that weight on his conscience to the grave; I wouldn't give him the chance to be free of his deceit. Any other decision wouldn't have made sense, we were old: Me almost fifty and him sixty. I thought about all of you, about the home I had so struggled to provide. I kept that pain deep in my heart. But from that moment on, I was never the same María de los Reyes...

I had two big pains at the bottom of my heart: my first heartbreak and your father's deception. They lived there together. When everything inside me went back to normal, I started to enjoy my imaginary infidelity without guilt, making love to the one who looked like Mella while having sex with your dad. After all, I had a right to deceive him too. Anyway, I'd never been unfaithful to him, I was single! I had always been a single woman!

But in the kind of reflection I'm doing now, this isn't the most important thing. Single or married. No, it's not so important. You've urged me to take stock of my life and in these moments, in spite of everything, I feel satisfied because I don't think I've wasted my time and I've confronted every problem life threw at me.

I've enjoyed living. There have been sad times and happy times. It doesn't grieve me to have lived! If I had to start all over again? I'd do it with pleasure, but with my own voice, in my own place, putting into practice all the experiences acquired through my struggle and my efforts. That would be worth it.

I'm not worried about whether I've acted well or not. I'll always live at peace with myself, because I believe I always did what I had to do. I have walked along with life, I haven't been left behind. And so, at ninety-four years of age, I feel good as new.

Life is reborn with every dawn and so am I.

Footnotes

1. All poems at the beginning of chapters are by the Cuban writer Georgina Herrera.
2. Derivation of *hocicuda* (big-snouted), used pejoratively to mean thick-lipped.
3. Literally to improve or advance the race.
4. Epiphany, the Twelfth day of Christmas, or the day the Three Kings, also known as Magi or Three Wise Men, who are said to have arrived in Bethlehem, bearing gifts for the infant Jesus; they are the Spanish and Latin American cultural equivalent of Santa Claus, bringing gifts to children on the morning of 6 January.
5. *Hechavarría* Family of Basque origin, first arrived in Santiago de Cuba in the latter part of the 17th century. Large land holdings dedicated to sugar production and other interests. By the 1760s they already possessed a sugar factory in the Morón district. In the middle of the 18th century they were, economically and politically, the ascendant patrician family clan in Cuba. At the beginning of the 19th century they colonized the Central Valley (Songo-La Maya). During the course of the 19th century their wealth declined somewhat and along with it their political power.
6. *Cabinda* Now a province of the Popular Republic of Angola, formerly part of the Kingdom of the Congo.
7. *Quicongos* Ethnic group belonging to the Bantu ethno-linguistic family. They occupied the northeast of Cabinda, between the Cuangoy river and the sea. Also called Congolese.
8. *La ley de vientres libres,* passed in July 1870, consisting of 21 articles by which slavery was masked. The first article stated that children born to slave mothers after the date on which the law came into effect would be declared free; nevertheless in article 6 it said that those freed by this law remained under the patronage of the owners of the mother, by which it can be understood that freedom was a relative concept.
9. *La guerra del '95* The War of 1895-98, also known as the Necessary War, was the last stage in the Cuban struggle against Spanish colonialism.
10. Marcus Garvey (1887-1940) Anti-colonialist Jamaican leader. Founder of the UNIA (United Negro Improvement Association), which aimed to unite all the black people of the diaspora and establish a country and government for and by them. Garvey travelled to Cuba in 1921, and

was allowed to make speeches in Havana as well as other cities. It was then that the Cuban branch of the UNIA was founded.

11. *Cocada*: sweetmeat made from grated coconut and sugar.

12. Parallel to the decline of the UNIA, the Jamaicans born in the country were recognized as Cubans with full rights, all of which contributed to the disappearance of the movement.

13. *Aponte* Named for the free black José Antonio Aponte who, in 1812, plotted an insurrection to overthrow the institution of slavery. When it was discovered, he was hanged, beheaded and one of his hands was chopped off and nailed to a wall in Havana.

14. Higher secondary education, pre-university.

15. Derogative term for a mouth with thick lips.

16. Literally improved or advanced, meaning with lighter skin and whiter features than their mother's.

17. Cuban insurgents who fought against Spanish domination.

18. *Yagua*: fibrous tissue at the top of the trunk of the royal palm, which naturally falls off every month; used for roofing and lining huts, wrapping tobacco etc. *Guano*: generic name for palm trees, other than the royal palm, and leaves which are also used for thatching roofs.

19. Traditional cuban stew.

20. Starchy tuber, similar to taro and yam. Known by various names throughout the West Indies, such as eddoe, dasheen, tanier, etc.

21. *Quilos* or *kilos* was slang for *centavos*, a small coin.

22. Popular name for Franco-Haitian dances brought to Cuba at the end of the 18ᵗʰ century. *Tumba* means dance in various Bantu languages.

23. Groups of dancers and musicians in carnival parades.

24. To go from one place to another moving rhythmically to music, eg. the conga.

25. *Pacto de Zanjón* Convention signed in 1878 between the representatives of the Colonial Spanish government and those of the Republic of Cuba in arms to bring the war to an end. Antonio Maceo rose up against this accord in an action known as the Protest of Baraguá.

26. *Ceuta* Spanish territory on the northern coast of Morocco, where they sent Cuban prisoners during the wars of the latter half of the 19ᵗʰ century.

27. *Tomás Estrada Palma* (1835-1908) First President of the Republic of Cuba, 1902-1906.

28. *Yunai* Popular pronunciation of the United Fruit Company, North American fruit monopoly that occupied the region of Banes and Antillas in the northern part of the former province of Oriente, from 1899 to 1960.

29. Insult meaning a (faecally) incontinent child.
30. *Escuelita paga* Modest, neighbourhood school where one teacher would give classes to all levels of primary age pupils for a small tuition fee.
31. Coin worth five centavos.
32. *Pedro Ivanet* Colonel of the Liberation Army, active participant in the Independent Colour Movement. Assassinated 12 July 1912.
33. *Evaristo Estenoz* Leader of the 1898 strike in Cuba. Member of the Bricklayers Union. Took part in the liberal uprising of 1906. Leader of the Independent Coloured Party. Committed suicide 20 May 1912, during the so-called *guerrita de los negros* (Little Negro War).
34. *Agrupación Independiente de Color* Founded 7 August 1908 by Evaristo Estenoz. Its leaders began to present the group as a Party with a very advanced social programme above and beyond discrimination problems.
35. *Martín Morúa Delgado* (1856-1909). Senator of the Republic for the Liberal Party. He was closely linked to the workers' movement, the Independence cause, and the Autonomist current. Debated the way in which blacks could best take advantage of their rights.
36. *José Miguel Gómez* (1858-1921). General of the Liberation Army. President of the Republic from 1909 to 1913.
37. *José de Jesús Monteagudo.* Head of the Rural Guard during the Gómez government.
38. *Mario García Monegal* (1866-1941). General of the Liberation Army. President of the Republic for two terms from 1913-17 and 1917-21.
39. *Fulgencio Batista Zaldívar* (1901-1973). Came to prominence in 1933 at the head of a sergeants' and soldiers' revolt. Elected President of the Republic for the term 1940-44. Staged a coup d'etat on the 10th of March 1952 and installed himself as dictator, from which he was overthrown by the Rebel Army. On the 1st of January 1959 he fled abroad, where he died.
40. Person who leads beasts of burden by the ring in their nose.
41. Person who transports large logs on carts pulled by oxen.
42. Booklet for noting down purchases made on credit.
43. Children's game, similar to Follow the Leader but in a spiral.
44. A sugar factory which, at that time, would probably have been an entire complex including a shop, clinic and school.
45. *La Virgen de la Caridad del Cobre* is the patron saint of Cuba. Legend has it that she appeared to three fishermen, whom she saved from a storm, early in the 17th century. Her shrine is in the village of El Cobre, in the province of Santiago de Cuba. She is one of the symbols of national identity.

46. Actually, she was Cuban.
47. Rubiera as well as his sister María Julia, had two brothers about whom he never spoke: Domingo Rufino, born in 1898 (unknown date of death, which occurred at a young age) and Rufino (1903-1929).
48. Could not have been Carlota since she had died in 1915.
49. María Julia did not actually die until 1980. It was later discovered that, although Rubiera had spent three months away from home, only half a day had been spent with his family in Cárdenas.
50. *Viejo.* literally 'old man' (*vieja* - old woman) used as a term of endearment among Cuban couples and friends of all ages.
51. *Don/Doña.* Terms of respect, now uncommon in Cuba, which once meant Master/Mistress.
52. Deep black skin colour.
53. Market Square.
54. Illegal game of chance.
55. Place where food is made and served to take home. In Cuba *cantina* means lunchbox or dinner pail.
56. Place where the practice of prostitution was disguised by dance.
57. Literally ducks, euphemism for effeminate or homosexual man.
58. *Jabado.* Light-skinned, red-head mulatto.
59. *Olga Guillot* (Santiago de Cuba, 1925) Singer of *boleros*, very popular in Cuba in the 1950s. She has lived in the United States of America since the triumph of the revolution.
60. *Celina and Reutilio.* A *campesino* or Cuban country music duo who came to popularity during the 1940s and continued performing until 1964. Celina González (1921) – continued her career, after the death of Reutilio in 1971 – known, in Cuba and internationally, as the *Reina del Punto Cubano*. In 1996, for the 50th anniversary of her life in the arts, she received the Picasso Medal awarded by UNESCO.
61. Cuban country music.
62. Two heavy wooden sticks which provide the central rhythm of much Cuban music.
63. Singers of a type of Cuban ballads called *trovas*.
64. *Ignacio Bombú* (1914-1973). Guitarist and singer from Guantánamo, lived in Santiago de Cuba from 1920 until his death.
65. *Benny Moré* (Santa Isabel de las Lajas, 1919-La Habana, 1963). Singer songwriter, his real name was Bartolomé. Idol of the Cuban people, internationally known as *El Bárbaro del Ritmo*.

66. In the cultures of many Spanish-speaking, Catholic countries, such as pre-revolutionary Cuba, a girl's fifteenth birthday party is a sort of coming-out ball.

67. A stimulating drink, typical of eastern Cuba, made of sugar and the leaves and roots of various plants.

68. *Agustín Lara* (1900-1970). Mexican songwriter and singer.

69. Radio contest.

70. *Partido Socialista Popular*. New name of the Communist Party after the dissolving of the Revolutionary Communist Union. Banned in the 1950s, it fused with other political forces after the triumph of the revolution: first in the Integrated Revolutionary Organizations and later in the United Socialist Party of the Revolution, which fed the present-day Cuban Communist Party (Marxist-Leninist party founded in 1965. Single party in existence in Cuba).

71. *César Vilar*. Communist leader since the 1930s. Active in the workers' movement.

72. *Noticias de Hoy* (Today's News) Official newspaper of the Popular Socialist Party.

73. *San Lázaro*. An image of Saint Lazarus, the leper, accompanied by dogs and supported by crutches, who is worshipped extensively among the Cuban people. In *Regla Ocha* (*Santería*) he takes the name Babalú Ayé.

74. To clear, divest or cleanse. Purificatory action that, according to believers, removes bad influences.

75. *Espiritismo cruza'o* (literally crossed spiritualism): Based on the fundamental religious concepts brought to Cuba by African slaves, syncronized with elements of Catholicism and the scientific spiritualism of Alan Kardec. The central nucleus is the belief in the impact – or lack thereof – of the spirits of ancestors in the development of the earthly life of human beings if these don't fulfil the ceremonies necessary for the eternal rest of the deceased in the afterlife. It is one of the forms in which homage is rendered to the dead, an expression of the indissoluble link between the invisible and visible worlds, where the former occupies the determining role, considered sacred to followers.

76. *Espiritismo de cordón* (literally cord spiritualism) : known by this name for the form of ritual. It contains many simplified elements of the Kardecian doctrine (see below), also of Catholicism and the so-called synchretic cults. The *cordoneros* effect cures using material elements, especially water, in sessions they call 'santiguación', which is where one finds the 'prestige' of the medium and which gives rise to its

dissemination. It is practised mainly in the provinces of Granma, Camagüey, part of Villa Clara and in the city of Havana.

77. Rub or knead out a stomach blockage or indigestion.

78. *Allan Kardec* (1804-1869). Synthesizor of the theory of scientific spiritualism. He wrote *Libro de los espíritus (Book of Spirits)* in 1857 and *Libro de los mediums (Book of Mediums)* in 1864 among others.

79. *Señorita,* in this case, means to imply virgin.

80. Literally, 'Here everybody *walks.' Caminar,* which usually means to walk, in this case means to go in search of solutions to problems with the help of the supernatural.

81. *Último rezo* (last prayer): Ceremony, which is the culmination of the nine days of mourning, in which the 'raising of the spirit' of the deceased is carried out.

82. Meaning heard and perceived things before they've happened with the help of the supernatural.

83. Complements given by person who has 'evil vision' with the aim of destroying the mentioned quality in the victim.

84. General purpose antiseptic, known by its brand name.

85. Adepts of the Afro-Cuban religion *Santería.*

86. Batista's security forces: the *guardia nacional.*

87. *Movimiento 26 de Julio.* Political group formed after the storming of the Moncada barracks on 26th July 1953, with popular roots in the teachings of José Martí. It directed the insurrection that brought down the dictatorship of Fulgencio Batista on 1st January 1959 in conjunction with other revolutionary organizations. Its actions were mainly carried out in the mountains of Oriente and Las Villas, as well as having a strong clandestine movement in the cities.

88. *Sierra Maestra.* Mountain range located in the eastern part of the country where, in 1956, under the leadership of Fidel Castro, the first guerrilla group was organized.

89. Games of chance

90. *Campaña de Alfabetización.* The 1961 Literacy Campaign eradicated illiteracy in Cuba.

91. *Crisis de Octubre.* Also known as the Missile Crisis, in 1962 the world was brought to the brink of nuclear conflagration It emphasized the firmness of the Cuban people in defending the gains of the revolution.

92. *Comité de Defensa de la Revolución.* Neighbourhood committees created in 1960.

93. Non-venomous Cuban snake which can grow up to 4 metres in length. Cuban boa or santamaría.

94. A small common Cuban snake, but seems to be used as synonym for majá in Oriente.

95. Bewitch, put under a spell, some *campesinos* believe that the majá can put its prey to sleep with its breath.

96. Song by Eusebio Delfín (Palmira, Matanzas, 1893- La Habana, 1965) Songwriter, guitarist and singer.

97. Traditional folk tale.

98. *Hurricane Flora*: disastrous hurricane that battered the former provinces of Oriente and Camagüey from the 4th to the 8th of October 1963.

99. *Milicias Nacionales Revolucionarios*. Organization founded in 1959 for the military preparation of the Cuban people.

100. Neighbourhood of Santiago de Cuba.

101. *Iyá* is the name of the largest of the three sacred drums of Santería. It is often personified as the 'mother drum' as in this chant: Iyá, the belly.

102. Lively, raucous party.

103. See note number 23.

104. Person who dresses up as a ridiculous figure for Carnival or the San Juan Festivals.

105. Person who wore the cape.

106. Traditional very substancial stew, made with goat meat.

107. Thick rounds of green plantain, fried, crushed and fried again.

108. Very thin chips of fried plantain.

109. *Mulatas de fuego* Group of very beautiful mulatta women in the 50s who took the spectacle of cabaret song and dance to the streets on carriages in the carnivals.

110. See note number 24.

111. *Carlos Gardel* (1890-1935) Internationally famous tango singer and movie star.

112. *Federación de Mujeres Cubanas.* Women's organization founded in 1961.

113. *La Coubre.* French freighter anchored in Havana harbour with a consignment of arms for Cuba. It was sabotaged and blown up 4 March 1960.

114. *Germán Pinelli.* Famous Cuban radio and television announcer and actor.

115. *Cementario Santa Ifigenia.* Cemetery of Santiago de Cuba and national monument.

116. See note number 55.

117. Light, loose shirt worn by Cuban men.

118. *María Valero* (1910-48) Spanish actress resident in Cuba. Protagonist of the most popular radio dramas of the forties especially *El derecho de*

nacer (Birthright) which could not conclude due to her tragic death in an accident. *Ernesto Galindo* Popular actor, protagonist of many radio dramas as well as the adventure series *Los Villalobos* and *Leonardo Moncada.*

119. Intricate hand woven open-work embroidery.

120. *Libertad Lamarque* (Argentina 1908) Actress and singer known as *la novia de américa* (America's Sweetheart). Very popular in Cuba.

121. Ornamental plant of the Aráceas family. In the eastern provinces of Cuba it is known as *malanga de la dicha* (lucky arum).

122. Character from a Laboulaye story, known in Cuba as *El camaroncito encantado* (The magic shrimp) from the José Martí version in *La Edad de Oro* (The Golden Age).

123. Or *casasola*, literally one who marries oneself.

124. *30th November 1956.* Date of the uprising in Santiago de Cuba and Guantánamo organized by the 26 of July Movement. It was meant to coincide with the landing of the *Granma* bringing Fidel Castro and his comrades to begin the struggle against the Batista dictatorship.

125. *Blanco es mi pelo, negra mi piel (White is my hair, black my skin)* directed by Marina Ochoa.

126. She's referring to the video about Reyita's life.

127. *Juan de Dios Peza* (Mexico 1852-1910) Romantic poet. Monologue cited originally entitled *Sola.*

128. *José Jacinto Milanés.* (Matanzas 1814-1863) Poet, dramatist, literary critic, novelist. The poem referred to is *La fuga de la tórtola (The turtle-dove's flight).*

129. *Gertrudis Gómez de Avellaneda* (Camagüey 1814-1873). One of the most important figures in Cuban letters. She wrote lyric and dramatic poetry, novels, short stories, legends, travel essays, journalism, an autobiography and many letters. The lines quoted are from the poem *A él (To him).*

130. *Luisa Pérez de Zambrana.* (Melgarejo 1835-1922) Distinguished figure of Cuban literature. She wrote poetry, and a novel, another was left unpublished.

131. *Amado Nervo.* (Mexico 1870-1919) Poet and prose writer.

132. *Julio Antonio Mella* (1903-1929) Cuban revolutionary and anti-imperialist. Founder of the Communist Party of Cuba, the University Students' Federation, the Anti-Imperialist League and the 'José Martí' Popular University. Symbol of the alliance between students, intellectuals and workers, he was assassinated in Mexico on orders of the dictator Gerardo Machado.

133. The title is *Canción para dormir a un negrito (Lullaby for a black baby)*. Published in the *Cuaderno de poesía negra (Black Poetry Review)* in 1938 by the poet Emilio Ballagas (Camagüey 1910-1954) during the period this author was developing within the current of black or *negrista* poetry. *Cuando tú sea grande va a sé boxeadó...* is the line Reyita quotes.

Further Reading

Andrews, George Reid. *Blacks and Whites in São Paulo, Brazil, 1888-1988.* Madison, WI: University of Wisconsin Press, 1991.

Bengelsdorf, Carolee. *The Problem of Democracy in Cuba: Between Vision and Reality.* Oxford: Oxford University Press, 1994.

Brereton, Bridget. 'Gendered Testimonies: Autobiographies, Diaries and Letters by Women as Sources for Caribbean History.' *Feminist Review* 59 (Summer 1998) 143-163.

Burgos-Debray, Elizabeth and Rigoberta Menchú. *I, Rigoberta Menchú: An Indian Woman in Guatemala.* London and New York: Verso, 1984.

Craft, Linda. *Novels of Testimony and Resistance from Central America.* Gainsville, Fla: University Press of Florida, 1997.

de la Fuente, Alejandro. 'Race, National Discourse, and Politics in Cuba: An Overview.' *Latin American Perspectives* 25:3 (May 1998): 43-69.

– 'Myths of Racial Democracy: Cuba, 1900-1912.' *Latin American Research Review* 34:3 (1999): 39-73.

Dilla Alfonso, Haroldo. 'The Cuban Experiment.' *Latin American Perspectives* 27:1 (January 2000): 33-44.

Dore, Elizabeth and Maxine Molyneux, eds. *Hidden Histories of Gender and the State in Latin America.* Durham and London: Duke University Press, 2000.

Eckstein, Susan Eva. *Back From the Future: Cuba under Castro.* Princeton: Princeton University Press, 1994.

Ferrer, Ada. *Insurgent Cuba: Race, Nation, and Revolution, 1868-1898.* Chapel Hill and London: University of North Carolina Press, 1999.

Gluck, Sherna Berger and Daphne Patai, eds. *Women's Words: The Feminist Practice of Oral History.* London and New York: Routledge, 1991.

Graham, Richard, ed. *The Idea of Race in Latin America, 1870-1940.* Austin: University of Texas Press, 1990.

Gugelberger, Georg M., ed. *The Real Thing: Testimonial Discourse and Latin America*. Durham and London: Duke University Press, 1996.

Halebsky, Sandor and John M. Kirk, eds. *Cuba in Transition: Crisis and Transformation*. Boulder: Westview Press, 1992.

Helg, Aline. *Our Rightful Share: The Afro-Cuban Struggle for Equality, 1886-1912*. Chapel Hill and London: University of North Carolina Press, 1994.

If Truth Be Told: A Forum on Stoll and Menchú. *Latin American Perspectives*, 26:6 (November 1999).

James, Daniel. *Dona Maria's story: Life History, Memory, and Political Identity*. Durham and London: Duke University Press, 2000.

Martinez-Alier, Verena. *Marriage, Class and Colour in Nineteenth-Century Cuba*, second edition. Ann Arbor: University of Michigan Press, 1989.

Marable, Manning. 'Race and Democracy in Cuba.' *Black Scholar* 15:3 (1984): 22-37.

Molyneux, Maxine. 'State, Gender and Institutional Change: The Federación de Mujeres Cubanas,' in Elizabeth Dore and Maxine Molyneux, eds., *Hidden Histories of Gender and the State in Latin America*. Durham and London: Duke University Press, 2000: 291-321.

Montejo, Esteban, *The Autobiography of a Runaway Slave*. Edited by Miguel Barnet. Basingstoke: Macmillan, 1993.

NACLA Report on the Americas Inside Cuba, 32:5 (1999).

NACLA Report on the Americas Cuba: Facing Change, 24:2 (1990).

Ortiz, Fernando. *Cuban Counterpoint*. Durham and London: Duke University Press, 1995.

Pérez, Jr., Louis A. *On Becoming Cuban*. Chapel Hill and London: University of North Carolina Press, 1999.

– *Cuba: Between Reform and Revolution*. New York and Oxford: Oxford University Press, 1988.

– 'Politics, Peasants and People of Color: The 1912 'Race War' in Cuba Reconsidered.' *Hispanic American Historical Review* 66:3 (1986): 509-539.

Perks, Robert and Alistair Thomson, eds. *The Oral History Reader*. London and New York: Routledge, 1998.

Safa, Helen I. 'Introduction.' *Latin American Perspectives* 25:3 (May

1998): 3-20.

Safa, Helen I. *The Myth of the Male Breadwinner, Women and Industrialization in the Caribbean.* Boulder: Westview Press, 1995.

Scott, Rebecca J. *Slave Emancipation in Cuba: The Transition to Free Labor, 1860-1899.* Princeton: Princeton University Press, 1985.

Stepan, Nancy Leys. *'The Hour of Eugenics': Race, Gender, and Nation in Latin America.* Ithaca: Cornell University Press, 1991.

Stoll, David. *Rigoberta Menchú and the Story of All Poor Guatemalans.* Boulder: Westview Press, 1998.

Stubbs, Jean. *Cuba: The Test of Time.* London: Latin America Bureau, 1989.

Stubbs, Jean and Pedro Peréz Sarduy, eds. *AfroCuba: Writings on Race, Politics and Culture.* London: Latin American Bureau, 1993.

Wade, Peter. *Race and Ethnicity in Latin America.* London and Chicago: Pluto Press, 1997.